READING INSTRUCTION IN THE SECONDARY SCHOOLS

BY

Henry A. Bamman

SACRAMENTO STATE COLLEGE

Ursula Hogan

EDUCATIONAL CONSULTANT

Charles E. Greene

FORMER SUPERINTENDENT OF SCHOOLS
DENVER, COLORADO

LONGMANS, GREEN AND CO.

NEW YORK · LONDON · TORONTO

1961

LONGMANS, GREEN AND CO., INC.
119 WEST 40TH STREET, NEW YORK 18

LONGMANS, GREEN AND CO., LTD.
48 GROSVENOR STREET, LONDON W 1

LONGMANS, GREEN AND CO.
137 BOND STREET, TORONTO 2

READING INSTRUCTION IN THE
SECONDARY SCHOOLS

PUBLISHED SIMULTANEOUSLY IN THE DOMINION OF CANADA BY
LONGMANS, GREEN AND CO., TORONTO

FIRST EDITION

LIBRARY OF CONGRESS CATALOG CARD NUMBER 61–6152

Printed in the United States of America

Foreword

More than eleven million students are enrolled today in secondary schools throughout our nation, seeking an education that will prepare them for more effective participation as citizens in our society. With the advent of missiles and interplanetary explorations, greater demands are being made on today's youth in terms of their fitness to become leaders and workers in a complex technological world. At no time in the history of our nation has there been greater stress placed upon education as the key to maintaining a position of pre-eminence on our planet. All eyes are turned on our school systems, both public and private, and wide scale investigations have been made with regard to the effectiveness of our curriculum. One of the critical areas in education has always been, and today is, reading.

This is a book on the teaching of reading in the secondary schools—both junior high schools and senior high schools. The school population with which secondary teachers are working is heterogeneous in aspirations, skills, experiences, aptitudes, and motivations. Therein lies a major problem. To provide all students with a common body of knowledge, necessary for the understanding and interpretation of civilization itself, to meet the demands of individual students, and to program a curriculum that will prepare young citizens for professional and technical positions, all secondary administrators and teachers are seeking more effective methods of learning. Reading has emerged as the most significant skill.

The training and experience of secondary teachers has not prepared them to cope with problems of divergence in the skills of reading. Investigations into the reading processes have indicated that each subject in the curriculum requires a body of basic reading skills, plus skills which are peculiar to that subject area. Thus, the responsibility for teaching reading skills lies heavily on each teacher in the secondary school.

In an attempt to provide the secondary school staff with a professional book on the teaching of reading, the authors have investigated all factors which are basic to a sound reading program. In this book consideration has been given to administration, organization, evaluation, methods, and materials; the teaching of reading in each of the major content areas is presented, with practical suggestions for the improvement of reading skills. Appendices list numerous aids and references for the teacher and the administrator.

January, 1961

H.A.B.
U.H.
C.E.G.

Contents

Contents

I

The Growing Importance of Efficient Reading

TODAY'S WORLD IS A READING WORLD! IN OUR American culture the amount of printed material accessible to the average person is enormous. The highway sign, the advertising pamphlet, the recipe book, the union and service-club news, the church bulletin, the daily newspaper, magazines, and numberless books all claim our attention and influence our thinking. Even the advent of sound movies, radio, and television has failed to displace the printed word and, in fact, has served to promote certain kinds of reading, such as drama or factual accounts of scientific phenomena.

To the American public learning to read well is of prime importance; and constant pressure is brought on schools to produce skilled and efficient readers. There are many reasons for this great public concern about reading instruction. In the first place, there is the prestige factor: the child or adult who reads poorly tends to lack status, and Mrs. Doe is greatly distressed whenever her young Johnny does not keep up with Joey Hocum next door. Second, reading is the tool by which pupils learn their various lessons throughout the elementary and secondary schools. Next, industry and the professions alike call for much reading on the part of working citizens as they go about earning a living. Last of all, the average citizen must read his papers, magazines, tracts, and books if he is to keep abreast of science and medicine, inventions, this season's improvements in cars or labor-saving devices, the latest capers or achievements of prominent citizens, the newest do-it-yourself hobbies, and dozens of other timely topics. The schools have good reason for making an earnest effort to promote high levels of reading proficiency on the part of their pupils:

A democracy demands of its education both *quantity* and *quality*. Never before have so many been educated so well as in the United States. These achievements have been the result of constant efforts to experiment, spurred by the desire to improve. The challenge of *quantity* has been largely met. Most of America's youth are in school and most classrooms have teachers. But the challenge of *quality* is now more difficult to meet than ever. . . . The body of knowledge that a secondary school must pass on to its students has expanded tremendously and is growing at a prodigious rate. Schools are frequently faced with obtaining the best possible results from financial resources that are too often inadequate. Efforts must be made to provide for the individual differences of the students and to determine which learning experiences are the most significant for the success of the individual. And education would fail to fulfill its purpose unless it also contributed toward the progress of society. A superior school today may be an inferior school a decade from now—unless bold, imaginative steps to improve *quality* are taken.[1]

[1] J. Lloyd Trump, *Images of the Future* (Urbana, Ill.: Commission on the Experimental Study of the Utilization of the Staff in the Secondary School, 1959), p. 5.

Importance of reading in today's world. In bygone days when printed matter was relatively scarce and social conditions were less complex than today, limited reading skills were a less crucial handicap. Modern man, indeed, finds that the ability to read comprehensively and critically is essential to his vocational, civic, and personal life.

The period since 1925 has been one of the most critical periods in our history. Within a relatively brief period of time, adults have faced a series of challenging economic, social, and political problems that have called for wide reading, clear thinking, and radical adjustments. The understandings needed have related to such matters as the soundness of our economic structure, the basic principles underlying our democratic form of government, the essential differences between various national ideologies, the causes and elimination of inter-group conflicts, the principles for which we fought during World War II, and the conditions that must be met to insure permanent peace. Because of the very character of the times, the demands made on readers have increased at an unprecedented rate.

In an effort to acquire needed information, young people and adults have read more widely and in greater numbers than ever before. As shown by numerous published reports, reading has continued to serve each of the vital purposes listed above. In addition, chief attention has been focused in turn on each of the successive problems which our nation has faced. Individuals have read widely and intensively to secure a clearer understanding of the issues involved and to search for possible solutions. In the course of time they have found it necessary to engage also in many other types of reading, the chief value of which was to provide release or to escape tension. Some sought to overcome their confusion and perplexities through wide reading in the fields of psychology, psychiatry, and other approaches to personality problems. Others turned to "Great Books" and to literature of "power" and "imagination." Such reading, it has been claimed, does far more than entertain, soothe, or inform. It gives direction to the thoughtlife of the reader, prepares him to see current problems in a broader perspective, and contributes to a full, rich and satisfying personal life.[2]

Development of twentieth-century reading programs. In spite of the fact that children and youth of today read as well as, if not better than, their parents and grandparents, public discontent with the current status of reading in our schools is all too evident.[3] In personal interviews and conferences, in magazine articles, and even in an occasional whole book the unease and criticism are expressed. A review of shifts in placement and emphasis on different aspects of reading instruction will give a background for understanding the developments in reading practices in recent years. This review will reveal why there are actually many high school students who are unable to read their textbooks with satisfactory ease and comprehension. Actually few students ever do reach their full reading potential;[4] and the high schools have a real task to perform if all pupils are to read as well as they should.

Until comparatively recent years the teaching of reading skills was considered the responsibility of primary teachers. That it is impossible to complete such instruction in the first three grades became evident as investigations were made into (1) the nature of the reading process and the developmental skills involved, (2) the skills lacking in the reading of middle-grade and junior high school pupils, (3) the

---

[2] William S. Gray, *Adult Reading* (1956 Yearbook for the National Society for the Study of Education), pp. 30–31.

[3] Ruth Strang and Dorothy Kendall Bracken, *Making Better Readers* (Boston: D. C. Heath and Co., 1958), p. 52.

[4] Paul D. Leedy, *Reading Improvement for Adults* (New York: McGraw-Hill Book Co., 1956), pp. 2–11.

course of child development. Taken together, the results of these studies showed that the primary child is too immature to acquire the most advanced types of skills and that certain skills must be introduced and mastered in the middle and upper grades, at the earliest. Over the past few decades schools have come to the general practice of teaching reading and study skills systematically as an integral part of the curriculum in the grades above the primary. Unless such instruction is provided, older pupils cannot handle the more difficult material and increasingly complex ideas with which they are expected to deal.

At about the time of World War II educators noticed that many secondary students were unable to read their textbooks sufficiently well. This unfortunate situation was partially the result of the growing tendency of students to stay in school until they were sixteen or more and of the growing practice of promoting slow-learning pupils into the high school, largely on the basis of chronological age. Nowadays practically every pupil continues into high school largely for the following reasons: there are laws establishing a minimum age for leaving school; employers increasingly demand that their employees have a high school education; there is a general cultural acceptance of high school graduation as a minimal educational goal. Consequently, the present high school population is extremely heterogeneous as compared with the selective group which was enrolled in high school prior to World War II.

While the general population has been growing in numbers during the past century, its growth has not been so spectacular as the growth in secondary school enrollments. From 1870 to 1930, the secondary school enrollment doubled every decade!

. . . A little deduction on your part will bring you to the conclusion that the increase in enrollments must have come in part,
a large part, probably, from those groups of our population
which had not formerly gone to high school. The United States
Office of Education reported that in 1952 seventy-five per cent of
all youth of high school age, 14–17, were enrolled in school. It
is estimated that the enrollment of all high-school-age youth who
live in cities is about ninety per cent.[5]

With the realization that many secondary students lack
the reading skills requisite for preparing their lessons, the
larger school systems began experimenting with continuous
developmental reading experiences for pupils for the entire
twelve-year span of the public school curriculum. Denver,
Los Angeles, Philadelphia, New York, and San Francisco
among others began an appraisal of the reading of students
throughout their systems. A typical example of the work
undertaken is shown by a publication issued by the San
Francisco Public Schools in 1946. For the junior and senior
high schools, the following statements were made:

d. In junior and senior high school, definite provisions should
be made for reading instruction as an integral part of the English
period. . . . The time required and the nature of the instruction
will be based on the students' needs and interests:

(1) His needs for additional skills to meet new demands
    in subject matter
(2) His need to learn the highly complicated, advanced
    skills for technical and professional reading
(3) His need for more drill in simple reading skills
(4) His needs for growth in reading ability to keep pace
    with his changing and maturing interests.

[5] Philip W. Perdew, *The American Secondary School in Action* (Boston:
Allyn and Bacon, 1959), pp. 15–16.

e. In addition to the definite provision for reading instruction in the English program, it is necessary for the teachers of other subjects to help students meet their reading needs as they occur in those subjects.[6]

For the high schools, many of the reading programs started out as "remedial" programs for retarded readers, but they have tended to expand into reading instruction for all students. This scattered experimentation gave convincing evidence that high school students do need continued practice in applying hitherto taught reading skills to their more difficult and complex assignments and that there must be, in addition, introductory teaching of high-level skills in interpretation and critical thinking. It was seen that even the brightest high school students needed such advanced reading instruction if they were to attain their potential reading level.

Unfortunate effects of reading deficiencies. In investigating the reading needs of the students high school faculties also became aware of definite relationships between inability to read well and behavioral problems; whether misbehavior was the cause or the result of reading difficulties was often hard to determine. These faculties felt a similar concern about the "dropouts" especially when they found how prevalent inability to read was characteristic of those pupils who had left school prematurely.

In a study of reading ability as it relates to the problem of dropouts in the high school, Ruth C. Penty investigated the situation in Battle Creek High School. Her findings corroborate what others had already reported: early leaving of

[6] *Teaching Guide: Kindergarten-Grade 12* (Curriculum Bulletin No. 201, San Francisco Public Schools, 1946), p. 11.

high school cannot be attributed to a single cause; there always appears to be a multiplicity of reasons, with marked inter-relatedness among them; low reading achievement *is* a factor operating in a high percentage of the dropouts. In Battle Creek High School more than three times as many poor readers as good readers left school before completing twelfth grade. However, not all poor readers left school, but were able to graduate in spite of their difficulties. These were young people who had achieved adequate emotional and social adjustment through moral support at home, their own deep interests, favorable school experiences, and lack of financial difficulties at home. These favorable factors induced them to put forth a real effort to complete high school.

Penty also investigated the effects of systematic remedial instruction in reading. She found that special help in reading skills caused more rapid growth in reading achievement than did incidental, unsystematic help. Also, the provision of special reading instruction tended to decrease the percentage of dropouts in the school poulation. She concludes with the following statements:

The past practice in most school systems of terminating special help in reading at the close of the sixth grade is not meeting the needs of students who are expected to read increasingly difficult and varied materials without receiving help in the techniques of reading these materials. The prevalence of drop-out in the tenth grade points to the need for special help in reading between the sixth and tenth grades. It is also undoubtedly desirable to continue the giving of reading help throughout the high school grades.[7]

[7] Ruth C. Penty, *Reading Ability and High School Drop-Outs* (New York: Bureau of Publications, Columbia University, 1956), pp. 72–77.

Developing sound programs of reading instruction. It is natural that there should be mistakes in the early attempts to cope with the poor reading of secondary students. Some of the pioneers in the movement to set up systematic programs knew little about reading skills and seized upon mechanical devices as the basic aids in improving reading. These "gadgets" seemed to offer an easy answer to problems of improving the students' reading; and their use became popular and widespread. However, recent research has shown that skills induced by the use of mechanical devices tend to be impermanent and not to carry over to any considerable extent to the reading of the printed page. They are seen as aids in a broadened program of reading instruction that utilizes much printed material specifically designed to build skills in word recognition, deducing word meanings, comprehension and organization of ideas, and critical reading.

No one type of reading program will fit the need of high schools in general. Each school must tailor a program suited to its particular group of students—their backgrounds, potential abilities, and needs for supplementary reading instruction. Its faculty must carefully analyze the local situation, set up a trial program, and continuously evaluate and modify it until a sound, workable plan has been evolved.

In planning a developmental reading program for secondary schools, certain guide lines should be observed. Some of the more important of these are presented here:

1. The program should be so planned as to meet the emerging needs of each individual student.
2. Each teacher in the school has a definite part to play in the program for building adequate reading skills.

3. The general types of reading skills should be developed and strengthened by direct teaching on the part of English teachers.

4. Each teacher of the content subjects must assume responsibility for introducing and practicing reading skills that are especially needed in the subject he teaches.

5. Each teacher should help students know how to study his subject most effectively and how to use reference materials particularly valuable in it.

6. Since students vary widely in interests and levels of achievement, every school must provide materials diversified in theme, treatment, and difficulty.

7. Some plan of grouping should be developed, on a flexible basis, so that students with comparable abilities, common interests, or identical needs can work together. There should be some provision for offering common experiences to the total group as, for instance, viewing films that deal with reading skills that all high school students should acquire.

8. There should be a program of continuous evaluation which utilizes a variety of instruments and procedures.

9. School faculties should acquaint themselves with the findings of investigations dealing with reading at the high school level and should be prepared to undertake further classroom research in order to establish sound practices and determine helpful kinds of materials for reading instructions.

It is encouraging to note how much time, thought, and energy many secondary teachers are devoting to setting up programs to improve the reading of their students. The typical high school teacher understands how heterogeneous the high school population has come to be, why it has become so, and why he has a responsibility for meeting the needs and interests of the students as they come to him for instruction. Any conscientious teacher stands ready to make all necessary adaptations so that he can provide adequate learning experiences for all youth, regardless of how widely divergent their interests and abilities may be.

How wisely and constructively the teacher has dealt with his students will become evident in future years as they assume their adult responsibilities as workers, heads of families, and citizens who may or may not be inclined and able to read with understanding and critical judgment about the conditions and problems that are confronting them at the time.

Sidney Head defines some of the conditions which today's high school teacher must keep in mind as he prepares his heterogeneous lot of students for intelligent living in their world. He writes:

> In former ages some publications—for example, the Bible or the works of Aristotle—certainly reached very large numbers of people in the course of time, but the elements of approximate simultaneity, low unit cost, and mass audience were lacking. A mass audience is not merely a large audience. It is an extremely heterogeneous audience, the members of which need have little in common beyond simultaneously receiving identical messages.[8]

Low-cost production of printed materials and heterogeneity of the reading public are producing the same problems of a mass audience that Sidney Head portrays in the field of broadcasting. Schools have a really serious responsibility for sending out into society literate, questioning, and informed young citizens. In the development of more critical and thoughtful readers lies the hope of survival of a democratic way of life.

This is the challenge to teachers in our secondary schools. How well will we meet it?

[8] Sidney W. Head, *Broadcasting in America* (Boston: Houghton Mifflin Co., 1956), p. 77.

Suggested Readings

GRAY, WILLIAM S. "Nature and Scope of a Sound Reading Program," *Reading in the High School and College.* 47th Yearbook, National Society for the Study of Education. Chicago: University of Chicago Press, 1948. Pp. 46–48.

Improvement of Reading in Secondary Schools. Bulletin 540, Texas Education Agency, 1953.

JEWETT, ARNO (ed.). *Improving Reading in the Junior High School.* Bulletin No. 10, U.S. Department of Health, Education, and Welfare. Washington, D.C.: Government Printing Office, 1957.

TRUMP, J. LLOYD. *Images of the Future: A New Approach to the Secondary School.* Urbana, Ill.: Commission on the Experimental Study of the Staff in the Secondary School, 1959.

WITTY, PAUL A. "Current Role and Effectiveness of Reading among Youth," *Reading in the High School and College.* 47th Yearbook, National Society for the Study of Education. Chicago: University of Chicago Press, 1948. Pp. 8–26.

The Suggestion Box

The implications of *Images of the Future* for the high school teacher are great. In a faculty discussion group, review this provocative publication. What implications are there for the teaching of reading and language arts?

In a preliminary planning session for the reading program, elicit from teachers their definitions of the word *reading*. Write down all the definitions given, and attempt to formulate a comprehensive definition. Compare this definition to Gray's "Criteria of an Effective Reading Program," quoted in the NSSE 47th Yearbook.

Ruth Penty's *Reading Ability and High School Drop-Outs* is worthy of a careful review by a member of the class or teaching staff. A random sampling of dropouts in the local school might be taken to determine what percentage of the dropouts was due to reading difficulties.

What has been the effect of mass media on reading habits and interests of young people? Consult the reports of the 1950 and 1960 White House Conference on Children and Youth.

II

Types of Reading Programs

IF THE READING PROGRAM IN ANY HIGH SCHOOL IS to be truly efficient it must be patterned to suit the particular plan the school follows in organizing its instruction. Some schools operate on the separate subject plan; others use the core curriculum; still others have a unified studies program. Reading programs, therefore, should vary from school to school.

Where a school operates in terms of separate subjects, responsibility for teaching reading skills tends to be scattered among the various subject departments. However, in the core or unified studies pattern of organization it is possible simultaneously to develop general reading skills and specific skills for a content area.

The Separate Subject Plan

Generally English teachers, under this plan, will assume responsibility for developing the general reading skills needed by high school students. Teachers in each of the other areas of the curriculum are expected to identify and teach the special reading skills demanded for reading materials in their respective areas. Chapter III is devoted to a discussion of the organization of the reading program, with particular emphasis upon identifying reading skills in the various content areas.

Reading as a part of the English program. How a secondary school operating under the separate subject plan organizes its reading program depends on how it groups its students. If they are classified into heterogeneous groups, there will be one kind of planning; if the policy is one of homogeneous grouping, another plan will be tried. However, no matter what the master plan of grouping, teachers find it advantageous to subgroup in terms of achievement level, potential ability to learn, or currently existing needs of the students. The program of reading instruction for each subgroup can then be definitely suited to the backgrounds, needs, and future plans of the students in terms of their vocational and educational prospects. The goal is to develop a reading program that will afford maximum opportunities for individual progress in mastering the needed reading skills.

Traditionally English teachers have a heavy work load; armloads of papers to read and correct each week, follow-up conferences, dramas and whole books and selections in weighty anthologies to present to pupils in such a way as to develop understanding and encourage a liking for good literature, oral discussion and storytelling to direct. The course of study of a typical secondary school outlines a huge body of content to be imparted to students. It is obvious that the English teacher must do careful planning and close scheduling if he is to cover all of this and "add" the teaching of general reading skills. Developmental reading appears to some English teachers an almost impossible addition to an already overcrowded curriculum. No wonder that English teachers ask "how to do," "when to do," and "what to do" questions about the reading program they are expected to conduct.

Organizing for instruction. There is no single best type of organization for a developmental reading program as part of the English curriculum. Each school faculty will have to make a careful appraisal of its practices in grouping, scheduling, selecting course content, and choosing instructional materials. English teachers must keep in mind the close relationship between reading and the other phases of English and make the utmost use of this relationship. Several major suggestions on ways of (1) organizing classes to include developmental reading and (2) carrying on instructional activities follow.

Experience has shown that more effective work is possible if groups for reading instruction are kept comparatively small. The practice of forming small subgroups provides more opportunities for children to ask questions, to participate frequently, and to interact with fellow learners. Besides, active participation tends to induce a kind of motivation and stimulation not possible in the greater restraint of a large group. Working with small groups also permits the teacher to choose materials that are appropriate for each cluster of learners, to devise a method or methods of instruction that will best awaken interest and provide lively incentives to learn, and to minimize the boredom for the rapid learner and the frustration of the slow learner that work in a large, unselected group is liable to promote. In the words of David Russell:

Many teachers believe that with three groups they can plan work which will more nearly fit the present reading achievement, the interests, and the potential reading growth of individual pupils than with one or two groups.[1]

Alcorn, Houseman, and Schunert suggest that teachers form subgroups within the class. Their reasoning is as follows:

The teacher may help one group while another works alone. Groups should be flexible so that the composition of the group being given instruction may vary as needed. It is unfortunate that a procedure which has been used with success, both at the elementary and high school levels, has been confined largely to the elementary school alone.[2]

Teachers in the secondary school, whether their groups represent the full range of ability from low to high, a limited range of average-to-above-average or of below-average-to-average, or an X-Y-Z distribution, should consider carefully the advisability of using subgroups.

Once the decision on the matter of grouping has been made, the teachers should proceed to select their materials and to plan promising methods of instruction. Several alternative plans of work follow:

Using a basic reading textbook with all students. If a single textbook is used with all students, teachers should develop a

1 David H. Russell, *Children Learn to Read* (Boston: Ginn and Co., 1949), p. 332.

2 Marvin D. Alcorn, Richard A. Houseman, Jim R. Schunert, *Better Teaching in Secondary Schools* (New York: Henry Holt and Co., 1954), pp. 231–32.

plan of differentiated assignments. For example, if the class is reading the story "Smoke over the Prairie" by Conrad Richter, students with the least reading ability might be held responsible for activities that demand this level of reading:

Know where the story took place
Know when it happened
Know what important event led to the problem
Understand the strategy used to get Mr. Gant away from the scene
Know the meaning of important common words: clamped, lathered, stale
Be able to tell the story in sequence.

The average group of readers would be expected to add to these points the following:

Characterize the principals in the story
Understand the historical period and recognize certain causes of the conflict
Appreciate the descriptive passages
Understand the meaning of some less usual, more difficult words: inciting, invariable, pervaded, ingratiate.

The most capable group of readers, in addition, would be asked to:

Select portions of the story that bring new insights into the difficulties associated with building railroads across the United States
Analyze the family problem
Select one of the characters and describe how they feel toward him
Adapt the selection for dramatization
Understand the meaning of all the words in the selection, with special effort to use the words in other contexts
Skim available reference books for supplementary information.

In the follow-up discussion the students who had reached the maximum part of the assignment would share with the slower workers who would be held responsible for doing well lesser portions of the assignment.

Using multitexts. Under the multitext plan the class would be separated into two or three groups, and the teacher would divide his teaching time among them. The total group might work together for a short period of ten or fifteen minutes on a specific skill needed in common; for example, a study of prefixes and words containing them, or skimming to find information, or improving oral reading through phrase reading, or finding examples of comparisons or contrasts.

Assignments for any group working independently must be definite and extensive enough to provide worthwhile learning activities for the full study period. A work sheet or study guide is probably the most efficient way of handling independent study periods. If one is used, there should be careful preliminary instruction on the use of a study guide.

While some students work independently in their subgroups, the teacher works with one group for whom he motivates the reading of a particular selection or guides a practice exercise, develops new vocabulary, asks questions and has the students skim for the answers, and makes a detailed assignment for ensuing silent reading. The plan of using multitexts with subgroups is an excellent one because pupils are encouraged to share their reading through audience situations or a discussion which brings out points of similarity or difference in the various selections that have been read.

Using a unified theme. This plan involves the use of different materials with each subgroup, although there is a common theme running through all. Then the groups may join in a discussion of this common idea. For instance, if the materials were to develop the idea of how individuals face personal handicaps, the discussion might bring out:

The effect of the handicap on the person
The relationship of time of life to the occurrence of the handicap
The persons who gave support or aid to the afflicted person
The greatest difficulties to be overcome
The final outcome.

While the materials used by all the groups of students would have a theme in common, the books would vary in difficulty so that Group I would read an easy book, Group II a book of average difficulty, and Group III a harder one. Before a final discussion by the joint groups the teacher might need to work with each group on a rotation basis. He would devote most time to the group needing the most help. If a teacher uses this unified theme plan, each subgroup can do intensive work with any materials it can handle successfully; later all groups can profit from sharing the different stories or articles and becoming acquainted with a wide array of authors and viewpoints.

An alternative of this plan is to provide a wide selection of titles with several copies of each title. Each student would then be free to select the book most appropriate and interesting for him. Those choosing the same book would form a "cluster" and work together.

Using self-selection of books. At the secondary school level there is a strong tendency for teachers to provide a wide variety of single titles so that students can select a book especially suited to their interests and reading levels. The use of self-selection entails careful planning and orderly administration on the part of the teacher. In the first place, he must be sure of an abundant supply of books and periodicals which cover a wide range of themes and levels of reading difficulty. At any one time there must be available a minimum of two books per student, and the reading level should extend from four grades below the class grade level to adult books. He should be assured of a constant supply of books for the year's work so that the offerings can be changed periodically without raiding or exhausting the supply of books for the school years to follow.

The individualized reading program can be successful only if the teacher holds conferences with each student on a scheduled basis so that he can determine the suitability of the material for the individual, the amount of progress the student is making, the depth of his understanding, and the need for instruction on specific reading skills. During the conference several phases of reading should be checked:

> The student's reaction to the selection
> His ability to relate what he has read
> Fluency in oral reading as he reads excerpts aloud
> His grasp of word meanings, particularly words with multiple
>   meanings or words defined in the context of the story
> His plan for future reading.

The teacher should make careful notes of any student difficulties. These may be discussed at the time of the conference and some specific suggestions given about materials and procedures to be used in practicing to overcome weaknesses. If several pupils need the same kind of help simultaneously, there is economy in forming a temporary sub-group to work together under the direction of the teacher. This "need group" may practice together until all members have mastered the needed skill or it may be necessary for the teacher to continue longer with some of the members than with others.

A special problem for the teacher in using this plan of self-selection is that he must guide each student in broadening interests and improving reading tastes. During the conference he must be sure to give sympathetic advice, wise guidance, and appropriate suggestions which will lead students (1) to increase their reading power through choosing materials which make gradually increased demands on their skills and (2) to choose books that give "meat for thought" as well as entertainment. Obviously, the teacher himself must be widely read and extraordinarily well prepared to direct such a program of self-selection.

Scheduling reading instruction. In a crowded schedule, fitting in periods for teaching the developmental skills sometimes seems a difficult problem indeed. No one seems to know the best way to provide time for such instruction, but the following suggestions may prove helpful:

1. *There may be an intensive period of reading instruction.* For instance, some teachers concentrate on developmental reading instruction for a period of six weeks at the beginning of a semester. If they do so, the instruction should be made very pointed by first determining the current achievement level and particular problems of the students and then giving exactly the instruction that will be of the greatest benefit. The teacher should especially keep in mind the reading demands to be met during the current school year and see

that the students get a good start in handling reading materials that call for new or more advanced skills.

2. *The instruction may be distributed over an extensive period.* A day or two a week may be designated as the regular time for reading lessons, sometimes a whole period and sometimes a part-period being saved for this purpose. The skills to be taught would be selected in relationship to the students' current needs and, in part, to the natural development order in which certain pyramiding skills should be developed. Skills that are being taught should be practiced in any other English lessons to which they are pertinent and the students encouraged to utilize the skills whenever appropriate in their lessons in other subjects. The practice of putting skills to work immediately is an effective one.

3. *The reading instruction may be introduced incidentally.* Under this plan the teacher stops in the midst of his other English teaching whenever the need for a specific reading skill becomes apparent in any of his English lessons. For instance, if the members of the class have failed to take advantage of a clear-cut contextual clue in interpreting a passage of literature, it would be considered a good time to have a lesson on the use of such clues; or, if students fail to take in the characterizations in a selection, the teacher may have them skim to find words and phrases that indicate the character's traits and then have the pertinent passages read aloud. Such instruction is certainly timely and likely to be impressive.

However, there is a danger of patchiness in incidental reading instruction. The teacher needs to have at hand a check list of the reading skills that are important in the students' general reading so that he may be sure he is including all requisite skills in his reading instruction. Such a check list is given in Chapter III. Probably a teacher should always take advantage of the timely use of incidental teaching, but should supplement this with systematic instruction at a regularly scheduled time.

The Core Program

The core curriculum emphasizes broad social problems or common learnings. Its purpose is to prepare all youth to participate in democratic living and to prepare them to contribute to continued improvement in civic and social conditions. The problems or themes chosen for study cut across subject-matter lines, sometimes with one particular subject making the greatest contribution to the solution of some problem (How do inoculations prevent the spread of disease?) and often with various subjects serving in about equal amounts (Do these books of fiction give a true picture of historical and geographical conditions?).

The core is assigned a large daily block of time in the schedule, usually three hours in grades seven, eight, and nine; and two hours in each of the three top grades. Within this scheduled time various kinds of activities take place, many of them calling for an extensive use of printed materials. As the students seek for definite information in their various reference books they may encounter difficulties in locating and understanding the passages that are pertinent. This is the time for the teacher to take note of reading handicaps and plan to work with groups or individuals to overcome these weaknesses. Since the kinds of difficulties tend to be numerous and varied, the teacher must have at hand a great variety of materials and must be prepared to employ many different techniques for introducing and providing practice on the needed skills.

In the core program students not only engage in the informational type of reading but do considerable recreational reading. The classroom teacher and the librarian can advisedly combine their efforts in enhancing the students' interest in varied reading materials. The librarian, for example, may prepare attractive book displays, assist each student in finding books that are exactly "right" for him, or give informal discussions about books and authors which deal with subjects pertinent to the core program or which afford high adventure or deep mystery for personal reading. For his part the teacher encourages frequent visits to the library for browsing and selecting definite types of books, provides free time for the students to interchange ideas and opinions of books, and displays his own genuine interest and enthusiasm for reading as a pleasant and profitable pastime.

The core teacher may schedule his time for reading instruction according to the same policies as those suggested earlier for English teachers. There may be relatively brief, intensive training early in the semester, regularly scheduled periods during the weeks of the school year, or irregular periods devoted to teaching at the time that need for a particular skill arises. Likewise, the materials for reading instruction may be selected and used according to the policies cited earlier: the same textbook for all with differentiated assignments to provide for differences in ability, cluster groups with different materials for each of the groups in terms of relative ability and current needs, multitexts featuring a common theme for all groups, and self-selection.

The Unified Studies, Subject Core, or Block Program

Many schools are organized with a subject core as the basis of instruction. In junior high schools a daily large block of time may be devoted to social studies, language arts, and science; social studies and the language arts; or science and mathematics. In the seventh grade the block of time is usually three hours; in grades eight and nine, two hours.

Under the unified studies plan the teacher meets two or three groups of students each day. This practice reduces the number of students with whom the teacher works (as compared with the customary four or more different groups each day); there is a corresponding increase in the amount of time to be spent with each group. Consequently, the teacher can more easily find time and opportunity for teaching the developmental reading skills, both generally and specifically helpful in the various subjects he teaches in the group. Such an opportunity is especially important in the secondary school years; it is the public school's last chance to build sound reading habits in tomorrow's adult citizens.

Typically at the secondary school level, the extended daily period is given over to a fused treatment of social studies and English. Literary selections parallel the topics under study in history, in either a thematic or a chronological sense. Thus the great persons and events of history come to life in the mind of a student; history takes on an emotional appeal; students learn that good historical fiction accurately reflects the social, economic, and political philosophies of the era; and that it may greatly clarify the great social conflicts and movements in recorded history.

Advantages of the unified studies program. From the

standpoint of setting up a program for reading improvement, the unified studies type of curricular organization offers several advantages:

1. The teacher has students under his direct guidance for a longer period each week than in a separate course plan of instruction; consequently, there is greater opportunity to assess the reading strengths and inadequacies of the students and to provide instruction to overcome difficulties and extend skills to higher levels.

2. The broad coverage of the reading materials that the unified program demands means that there is likely to be the "right material for the right student" at hand at any particular time. The most capable students may be making an intensive study of some richly rewarding side issue, while the class plodders are reading to get the essentials in simpler books and periodicals.

3. The extended-day period gives the teacher much opportunity to teach reading skills directly and to demonstrate specific application of such skills to different kinds of materials which are used in the subject areas of the unified program.

4. Unified studies, because of the length of the period and the smaller number of students per teacher, give opportunities for more effective grouping of students in order to meet their specialized interests and needs.

Informal Coordination of Content Areas
for Skills Development

In the absence of the core or the unified studies program, it is highly desirable that the various teachers of the content subjects coordinate their reading instruction. Chapters VIII through XIII deal specifically with the teaching of reading in the various content areas; but actually it is unwise for each teacher to operate separately. There is so much chance for needless duplication as students manifest similar needs in each of several subjects at the same time. The principal or one of the teachers should take the lead in coordinating the reading program whenever the school curriculum is organized in terms of separate subjects.

Some schools have successfully organized a school-wide reading program by selecting a responsible teacher from each content area to serve on a central reading committee. This committee examines the various courses to determine which reading skills are common to all areas and which are particularly applicable to each subject area. Presumably the English teachers would assume responsibility for the more generalized skills, and the content teachers would divide the remaining skills among themselves in accordance with the importance of each skill to a special content area.

In regard to the general skills, the entire faculty should sit down together and discuss the list which the committee has set up. Then the teachers from each area should explain to the English teachers just how each skill operates in their respective subjects. In addition, the teachers of the content areas should meet periodically to talk over the specialized reading skills that are currently important. And it may well be that the same students are needing the same reference and study skills in two or more content subjects at the same time. Then the teachers can make some sensible "division of labor" and, more important, still reinforce one another's teaching.

Also, since the students' writing, speaking, listening, and reading skills are interdependent, suggestions for fostering growth in the respective skills should be exchanged among the teachers; they should also agree regarding the standards to which the students should be held in their work, regardless of the content area.

School faculties who take seriously their responsibility for teaching the developmental reading skills rather typically call in a reading specialist to help them work out a coordinated reading program. Often such a specialist is on the central staff of the school district; there is almost sure to be a highly qualified person on the faculty of a nearby college for teachers. Teachers in the secondary school are likely to be unfamiliar with materials and methods for teaching reading skills and therefore will profit greatly from the opportunity to work with a specialist in reading.

The Reading Laboratory

As has been shown, current practices in promoting pupils and in retaining them in school until they are sixteen or more years of age have meant that many retarded readers reach the high school. Such students may need expert help if their reading is to improve, and few high school teachers are prepared to give such help. To meet this problem, some high schools are organizing a special reading laboratory for their retarded readers. If such a laboratory is to be successful, certain conditions must prevail. Here are some of the major ones:

1. There must be sufficient space available, separate from rooms devoted to other school functions.

2. A competent reading specialist who understands the whole gamut of reading skills must be put in charge.

3. A wide variety of materials, from all content areas, must be available in the laboratory.

4. Administrators, counselors, and teachers must agree on a policy regarding the *type* of difficulty to be treated in the laboratory. It must not become a dumping ground for the "problem" students who are weak in reading skills but have little potential for improvement and who will profit more from good counseling, a vocational program adjusted to their abilities, or work in special classes.

5. Whatever training the laboratory provides should be systematically followed by the teachers in the school. Every responsible member of the school staff should know what is being done for each student and every teacher should see that the skills that are being taught are put to use in the regular classroom. Transfer will take place only as the school staff makes a direct effort to have the work of the laboratory applied to the various lessons of the day.

6. The reading specialist should be given an opportunity to give extended in-service training to the teachers in the school. All students need reading instruction of some sort; and the reading laboratory can care for only the promising students who have serious reading problems. The teachers have a heavy responsibility for building the reading skills that all students need.

7. Each student who needs specialized help in the reading laboratory should be given released time in his schedule. He must not be permitted to feel that attending special classes in the laboratory is a penalty, but rather an opportunity to work toward his reading potential and to become a

better reader. He should also feel a responsibility for putting forth his best efforts in an attempt to improve his reading skills.

8. While the reading laboratory is largely geared to work with the retarded reader who has capacity to improve, there should also be provided training for superior students who need to develop advanced skills for doing the specialized reading of which they are capable.

9. Adequate funds must be made available to the reading specialist for the purchase of materials and equipment, clerical help, and student or faculty assistants.

Summary

The following points have been made in Chapter II:
1. The way the high school is organized for instruction will largely determine the kind of reading program it should have.
2. It is desirable to have some plan for grouping the students within the classroom.
3. If the English department assumes the major resonsibility for teaching the general reading skills, one of the following plans may be followed:
   a. Differentiated assignments based on the same text
   b. Having independent groups which use different texts
   c. Centering materials about a unifying theme, with different texts for each of several groups of students
   d. Providing self-selection on a completely individualized basis
   e. Organizing self-selection around a unifying theme.
4. The development reading program may be handled intensively over a brief period of time, extensively by providing spaced periods over a semester or year, or it can be

incidental with skills taught as needs arise in literature or the content subjects.

5. In core or unified studies programs there is a wide choice of reading materials; instruction on general and specialized reading skills can be concomitant as students work with both English and the content areas in the same class.

6. Teachers in the content areas are responsible for teaching the specific reading skills demanded by their respective subjects; they should also cooperate with the teacher of developmental reading by indicating the current general reading needs of the students.

7. The reading laboratory, with a reading specialist in charge, cares for promising students who are weak in reading skills and for superior students who need more advanced instruction in reading skills.

8. The reading specialist should give in-service training to other teachers in the materials and methods of reading instruction at the secondary school level so that they can give more effective guidance to students' reading in textbooks, references, and literary books.

Suggested Readings

FALK, PHILLIP H. "The Role of the Administrator in Providing Adequate Reading Materials in Schools and Classrooms," *Materials for Reading*. Supplementary Educational Monographs, No. 86. Chicago: University of Chicago Press, 1957. Pp. 197–202.

FAY, LEO C. "Basic Principles Underlying the Instructional Program," *Reading in the High School: What Research Says to the Teacher*. Bulletin No. 11, National Education Association. Washington, D.C.: The Association, 1956. Pp. 11–13.

————. "Organization of the High School Reading Program," *Reading in the High School: What Research Says to the Teacher*. Bulletin No. 11, National Education Association. Washington, D.C.: The Association, 1956. Pp. 9–11.

JENSON, T. J. "Staff Cooperation in Improving Reading," *Reading in the High School and College.* 47th Yearbook, National Society for the Study of Education. Chicago: University of Chicago Press, 1948. Pp. 294–314.

PELLETT, ELIZABETH A. "New Approaches to Grouping in High School," *The Reading Teacher,* XI (December, 1957), 109–15.

The Suggestion Box

Teacher "readiness" for the reading program is extremely important; together the teachers should appraise their current practices in grouping, scheduling, selecting course content, and choosing instructional materials. In terms of the organization of the local secondary school, how can adaptations be made in order to set up a good reading program?

What implications does Trump's *Images of the Future* hold for reorganization of the instructional program to include instruction in reading skills in all content areas?

For a period of one week each teacher of a subject area lists each time he makes reference to reading and related language skills and the number of times instruction is given in these skills. In a staff meeting a comparison of each teacher's diary for the week should reveal overlapping of teaching emphases and occasional omissions.

A group of staff members should investigate and observe existing reading laboratories or corrective reading programs in other secondary schools and report in detail their conclusions to the other staff members. Using the criteria suggested in this chapter for setting up a reading laboratory, is it possible to initiate such a program?

III

Organizing the Reading Program

BECAUSE SECONDARY TEACHERS FEEL A GROWING concern about the quality of their students' reading and are coming to the realization that it is impossible to complete reading instruction in the elementary school, there is a steadily increasing belief that a developmental reading program should be an integral part of the secondary school curriculum. However, belief is one thing; actual organization and execution of a definitive plan is another. There are many hurdles in the way of secondary school faculties who seek clear and well-defined procedures in getting a reading program under way. The first step is to analyze carefully the current practices shown in the check list on pages 36 and 37.

Setting up policies. In the initial stages of planning a reading program the teachers and administrators must think through certain problems. The check list below will aid them in defining some problems. Others which will need to be considered are listed here and will be discussed in this chapter:

Is our school's reading program to be designed for *all* students?

Is it to be primarily developmental or corrective?

Will the entire faculty be involved, or will specified members assume the responsibility?

Can we use the present counseling and testing program to make a correct and thorough identification of the reading skills that are weak and the students who need help, or must there be supplementary means of determining the reading needs of our student body?

Who, if anybody, on our faculty is competent to take the lead in setting up and administering the reading program our school needs?

Are the members of the faculty sufficiently informed in the area of reading skills to give the necessary instruction; or must we have in-service education to provide sufficient preparation?

Are the proper instructional materials adequate, other than the regular textbooks and usual library holdings, to meet the diversified needs of the students to be enrolled in the reading program?

Should we introduce the high school reading program a grade at a time; or should we launch all levels into the program simultaneously?

Should there be a special reading laboratory; or should all the reading instruction be given in a regular classroom?

If a comprehensive reading program is to be set up, the faculty of the entire school must eventually be involved. However, it is possible to begin in a smaller way. All sorts of beginnings are possible. Actually who should take the initiative? It may be a single teacher or the group of teachers who are concerned with a certain subject area; a department

Check List of Reading Practices in the Secondary School

	Very Well	Fairly Well	Not Well Enough	Not At All
I. Is provision made for continuation of the teaching of reading skills throughout the grade levels of the secondary school?				
—Do faculty members accept responsibility for orienting themselves to the reading program of the elementary schools?				
—Does each teacher plan for teaching the reading skills as an integral part of his subject matter?				
—Does each teacher recognize the reading problems which are involved in his subject areas?				
—Are provisions made, in each subject area, for meeting the needs of students who have a wide range of abilities in reading?				
—Are provisions made for a wide range of reading interests, in terms of both materials and instruction given?				
—Have the faculty members agreed as to the scope and sequence of skills to be emphasized at successive grade levels?				
—Are the study skills and habits pertinent to the various subject areas clearly defined and do teachers assume responsibility for helping students develop more efficient study habits?				
—Are materials, personnel, and space available for a laboratory program for the retarded readers?				

II. ~~Are materials adequate and consistent with the kinds of programs~~ offered?

—Is there a wide range of periodicals, books, magazines, newspapers, and pamphlets for each subject area?

—Are materials sufficiently varied in terms of interests and reading levels of all students?

—Are materials adequate for the recreational needs of the students?

—Is guidance given, in each subject area, in the use of reference materials and textbooks?

—Are materials provided for the student who wishes to practice and develop better reading skills?

—Do trained personnel assist students in the location and use of reference materials?

III. Is there an adequate program of evaluation?

—Are the results of standardized tests made available to all the teachers—both total and subscores?

—Are the teachers apprised of the reading levels of their students?

—Do the standardized tests which are used cover adequately the skills needed for reading in each of the content areas?

—Are students apprised of the results of evaluation?

—Are provisions made through the counseling services for diagnosing cases of extreme reading disability?

—Do counselors provide opportunities for the students to discuss their study and reading problems?

—Are provisions made for superior students to seek, on a voluntary basis, extension of their reading skills?

head or a librarian; members of an entire department; a principal, the curriculum director, or the school superintendent; or a consultant working with a group of teachers in a unified studies program. It is even possible for a single teacher to work independently in his own classes, since success in this small beginning of a reading program may interest his fellow teachers. The ultimate goal, of course, is a united, well-organized effort with good leadership which functions continuously through constant planning and careful evaluation.

Just as the students themselves read best when the reading assignments are related to their experiences and interests, so is it true that the teachers who are launching into a developmental reading program should receive assignments suited to their personal backgrounds and interests. Then they may experience a real sense of involvement and see how they can serve effectively in the school-wide effort to improve the students' reading. Without a feeling of genuine concern and involvement, teachers will scarcely do an effective job.

Involving teachers in the reading program. Because teachers in the secondary school specialize in certain curricular areas when they prepare to teach, they are likely to be more heterogeneous than a typical group of elementary school teachers who expect to teach all or most of the phases of the curriculum. Consequently, many secondary teachers know little about the teaching of reading and frequently feel no responsibility for guiding their students' reading. Reading is somebody else's business—business that is all too poorly done, in the estimation of such teachers.

A good way to involve all the teachers in the high school in a program to improve students' reading is to ask each teacher to list the reading needs he notices in his classes.

Subsequent classification of these lists will clearly demonstrate that some of the needs are common to all areas of the curriculum, and that others are more or less restricted to a particular subject area. As an instructor thus takes part in identifying the reading needs that are peculiar to his subject he is likely to become interested in the reading problems of his students and to be willing to take an active part in improving skills that are important in his subject. The check list on pages 40, 41, 42 suggests reading and study skills which the teacher of a particular subject might use to determine the relevancy of skills to his subject and the competencies of his students in those skills.

Involving students in setting up a program to improve reading. Today's youth are growing up in a "new world"— a world of unprecedented exploits, one of disturbing conflict and uncertainty. To render maximum assistance to present-day secondary students, teachers must fully realize the demands that are being made upon each young person. Peter F. Drucker in his provocative article, "America's Next Twenty Years," emphasizes that

. . . Even in routine jobs automation will require ability to think, a trained imagination, and good judgment plus some skill in logical methods, some mathematical understanding, and *some ability well above the elementary level to read and write.*[1]

At the secondary school level it is important that teachers lead students to recognize that underlying all effective reading is the necessity for having a purpose for reading. Whether his purpose be to find relaxation and recreation or to seek insight into a personal problem, the reader must establish

[1] Peter F. Drucker, "America's Next Twenty Years," *Harper's,* CCX (April, 1955), 45.

A Check List of Reading and Study Skills for the Content Areas

Subject: _____

Teacher: _____

Skills	Relevance to the Subject				Status of Students		
	Very Important	Important	Of little Importance	Of no Importance	Superior	Adequate	Poor
WORD-ATTACK SKILLS							
1. Phonetic attack on new words							
2. Knowledge of inflectional endings							
3. Use of context clues for pronouncing new words							
4. Knowledge of principles of syllabication							
5. Knowledge of compound words							
6. Extensive sight vocabulary							
7. Recognition of prefixes, suffixes, and roots							
WORD-MEANING SKILLS							
1. Understanding of technical terms							
2. Use of the dictionary							
3. Use of the glossary							
4. Use of new terms in speaking and writing							

5. Understanding of prefixes, suffixes, and roots
6. Understanding of figurative language
7. Understanding of personal and general connotations of words
8. Understanding of technical vocabulary related only to this subject

COMPREHENSION SKILLS

1. Recognition and understanding of main ideas
2. Recognition of relevant details
3. Recognition of relationships among main ideas
4. Organization of ideas in sequence
5. Understanding of time and distance concepts
6. Following directions
7. Reading maps, tables, and graphs
8. Distinguishing between facts and opinions
9. Judging and criticizing what is read
10. Reading widely to seek additional evidence
11. Drawing inferences
12. Listening attentively and critically

STUDY SKILLS

1. Using textbooks efficiently
2. Using the library efficiently
3. Taking notes
4. Scheduling time efficiently

41

A Check List of Reading and Study Skills for the Content Areas (continued)

Subject: _____   Teacher: _____

Skills	Relevance to the Subject				Status of Students		
	Very Important	Important	Of little Importance	Of no Importance	Superior	Adequate	Poor

STUDY SKILLS

5. Preparing for examinations
6. Preparing for discussions and reports
7. Using reference materials efficiently

MECHANICAL SKILLS

1. Adjusting rate of reading to suit purpose and content
2. Reading orally
3. Reading selectively
4. Skimming with a purpose

INTERESTS

1. Developing new interests
2. Developing wide interests
3. Shifting interests without losing motivation

for himself why he is reading. Teachers must in many cases take considerable responsibility in establishing such purposes for the immature youngster, not on the basis of "I know what's best for you" but from the standpoint of his willingness to share his more mature judgment in discussions designed to establish purposes suitable and acceptable to young people.

One good way to ensure the success of a school-wide program for improving reading skills is to involve the students in its planning. As they discuss the need for such a program and the values that can be achieved through it they are most likely to share in and to accept plans for it and to become enthusiastic participants. For instance, the college-bound student is most certainly impressed today with the necessity for being able to read well enough to pass entrance examinations, and it is often this student who is most highly motivated to improve his skills.

To a sensitive teacher, work with adolescents is a great challenge: they are, on the whole, capable and eager to learn; they are active, inquiring, and alert; they are interested in adding to their store of knowledge through vicarious as well as firsthand experience. These are the years when friends, out-of-school interests, television, and movies typically absorb much of the adolescent's time; if he is to give reading instruction a place in his full schedule, it must significantly contribute to his welfare by satisfying his immediate needs and adding to his efficiency. If certain students should continue to be reluctant to share in the reading improvement program they should not be forced but tactfully and gradually introduced to materials and activities that will show immediate results in easing their reading problems.

Heavy and widespread demands for efficient reading.
Because the high school curriculum is exploratory, much
reading is required. Every subject opens up a new world
of knowledge and action through enlightening initial experiences, or at the very least it broadens already familiar
fields through revealing entirely different perspectives from
those seen in earlier school years. All these new curricular
opportunities call for much reading in every subject. All
secondary school teachers, therefore, have a definite responsibility for helping their students to read effectively and
extensively in their respective content areas.

Some teachers of the so-called academic subjects are
inclined to think that only in their fields is it necessary for
students to carry on an extensive reading program. Other
teachers of the more technical subjects, or of subjects requiring a great deal of computation or manipulation of a mechanical nature, tend to feel that they have little or no responsibility for guiding their students' reading, since reading seems
to be relatively unimportant in these technical subjects.
Actually the students' reading is important to learning in all
subjects in the curriculum. It is obviously crucial in the social
sciences and literature; but physics, chemistry, home economics, algebra, vocational agriculture, and others require
thoughtful reading too. In order to understand the principles
of electricity, students must read. Reading recipes and directions on dress patterns in home economics, reading specification sheets for building a desk or table in industrial arts,
and reading problems and theorems in algebra and geometry
call for genuine skill in word recognition, word meanings,
comprehension, and critical thinking. The students' general
competency in any of these subjects is dependent on their
ability to read efficiently.

The administrator's responsibilities. Once a group of teachers has come to realize the heavy demands that their subjects make on the students' ability to read and they have accepted their responsibility for improving reading skills, they must receive the active support of their administrator and his staff. As a first step the administrator group must familiarize itself with the features of a sound reading program at the secondary school level. Next, through staff discussions and in-service meetings this group should develop the administrative guidelines of a reading program suited to the local situation and set up a definite scheme for getting the program under way. As an educational leader the administrator may encourage pilot programs, the development of reading guides in each subject area, and in-service workshops to help teachers understand how to guide the students in mastering all needed reading skills. Still another responsibility he must assume is to make available to teachers and students an adequate supply of reading materials in all subject areas; he should also think through and set up the channels of communication whereby the teachers in the various departments would share their experiences and findings with their fellow workers in the entire faculty. Finally, he should supervise his teachers in a continuous evaluation of the reading program so that modifications may be made advisedly as more and more effective ways of building up the students' reading skills come to light.

In the Folsom Unified School District of Folsom, California, the high school principal (a former elementary school principal) has initiated a highly successful reading program for all students in the high school. With rare insight into the reading problems of youngsters who enter the high school, this principal consulted with a county schools consultant, a college instructor, his counseling staff, and his teachers before he started to set up guidelines for the program. A highly skilled elementary school teacher, with good training in library skills, Mrs. Lillian Culver was selected to reorganize the school library as a center for the teaching of reading and study skills. All students in the high school were tested on standardized tests for achievement and intellectual capacity; the counselors met with each student and discussed test results and made recommendations for improvement in reading and study skills. The choice of participating in the program was left to the student. Mrs. Culver has conducted classes in study and reading skills each period of the day; those students who suffered mainly from lack of study skills have made rapid progress and have returned to their regular classroom program. Students with critical problems in reading have been instructed in small groups of no more than six students in each group. Self-selection of materials has been encouraged and guided; individual instruction in particular skills has been given as needed. The teachers of content areas have become increasingly aware of the reading needs of their students and are cooperating in this skills-development program. This program serves as an example of the influence of a perceptive administrator.

It is obvious that planning a reading program requires extra time, and something in the crowded schedule of the secondary teacher must be adjusted. Here the administrator can set aside a period a week for meetings and discussions, arrange for substitute teachers to take over while the regular teacher is involved in planning the reading program, or arrange student activities in such a way that teachers are actually free for planning. The average teacher in the secondary school is already overburdened; unless some arrangements are made at the administrative level to free that teacher for working on the reading program, the program simply will not succeed.

Advisability of adequate communication. If a school-wide program in the secondary school is to be truly successful there must be ample opportunities for the teachers to share and evaluate together their experiences in the program. They must come to a clear understanding of whether it is to be a developmental or a remedial program; whether regular textbooks or special materials are to be used; whether the goals are immediate or long-range. As the teachers discuss their materials and procedures they will perceive the shortcomings as well as the productive features of the program. As they work at developing and carrying out the program they can also contribute to simple handbooks or guides helpful to fellow workers. Also, all members of the faculty should seek, through current periodicals and new books, to keep abreast of the reports on research and current practices in reading programs and to bring back to their fellow workers the ideas that are pertinent and constructively suggestive for the local school's reading program.

There should be a consistent effort to keep parents informed about the developments in the reading program. Otherwise they may share the nationwide concern about the inadequate reading abilities of the youth of today and engage in destructive criticism that is unjustified and would not occur if the school faculty had helped them to know and understand the reading program which the local teachers have been developing. Parents tend to support any constructive school practice of which they are informed and which they understand; they may fail to support one they do not understand or may strongly criticize an efficient school staff if they are uninformed about the good work that is going on.

Use of resource personnel. It may well be that a school system that is planning to initiate a program for the improvement of the reading skills will discover that no one on the administrative or instructional staff is actually trained in the teaching of reading. In such a situation there should be employed a reading consultant who can act as adviser, leader, and model teacher in the new program. There may, however, be one or more persons on the staff who are qualified to give leadership to the program. If so, such persons should be freed of some of their regular responsibilities so that they will have time to devote to planning and administering the reading program. Well-qualified teachers may be released entirely from their former duties; those less fitted for leadership may do an adequate job if a part-time consultant from a nearby college is employed to give leadership in the planning sessions and to direct an in-service workshop for the entire high school faculty. Some schools have encouraged interested teachers to take summer courses at colleges and universities to prepare themselves as leaders in the secondary reading program.

In the Washington Unified School District of West Sacramento, California, a reading program for the secondary schools has been initiated through the efforts of the coordinator of secondary curriculum, the assistant superintendent in charge of instruction, the principal of the high school, and numerous key teachers. At the nearby state college three of these people participated for a semester in a seminar on the teaching of reading in the high school; concurrently, meetings were held by these people with groups of teachers in the various content areas of the high school. During the following semester, a reading specialist from the college conducted a series of meetings for the entire staff of the high school, defining reading needs, discussing skills development in the content areas, and discussing guidelines for a threefold program: remedial, corrective, and accelerated. The meetings with the specialist were held monthly; between meetings discussions were conducted in the district with groups of teachers from content areas in an attempt to plan carefully for a future program. Two teachers in the district (one a former elementary school teacher) elected to take course work at the college in the diagnosis and remediation of reading difficulties. This program has moved slowly but carefully toward the development of a philosophy of reading for *all* students.

Levels of reading proficiency to be sought. As has been shown, many students of mediocre ability are enrolled in the high schools of today. They typically read too poorly to be successful with the advanced materials which they are supposed to read in secondary courses. While the teachers should find means of providing simpler materials for such students, they should also work at bringing the young people up to a reading level that will enable them to do the essential reading of adult out-of-school living. They must be able to read well enough to gain vocational respectability in that they can read simple signs and directions, fill out applications for employment or drivers' licences, or follow specifications for a particular job. The teachers should see to it that the high school reading program affords opportunities to do reading tasks of the practical type.

Unfortunately there are many poor readers who will be going to college because of family ambitions or because they themselves will finally wake up to the desirability of being educated for the leadership they are really potentially able to give. However, many such secondary students merely want to "get by," to pass a course without "cracking a book," to devote their major attention to sports and a good time generally. Many highly intelligent young people who have achieved satisfactory grades in high school by depending on their superior ability to observe, to call on past experience, to listen critically, and to talk volubly "off the top of their heads" are ill prepared to read with fluency and depth when they first enter college courses that are truly demanding on good reading skills and study habits.

Teachers in the secondary school must feel a deep concern for any students who have high potential but read poorly. First of all, such students must be identified, their weaknesses discovered, and a remedial program laid out. The hardest task of all may be to interest these students in improving their own reading. Some measures for motivation are (1) revealing to a student his actual potential and the strong possibility for his improving in reading; (2) starting with some simple and practical measures that are likely to bring speedy improvement, such as learning how to use topical headings as an aid in finding main ideas in a history text; (3) giving speed exercises on relatively simple materials and having the student keep a graph to show his gain in rate; or (4) bringing in simple books related to his hobbies and interests. There are other fruitful measures that will be discussed in detail in later chapters. The point is: it is important to involve the high-potential low-achiever in a helpful reading program. It will pay big dividends.

Then there are those students who already read well but need guidance in acquiring the more advanced skills that high school courses call for. Here a truly developmental reading program is essential—one that builds on an elementary school curriculum that has adequately done its reading job to the extent that the children were mature and able enough to master the skills appropriate at the grade school level.

One consideration that should constantly be kept in mind is: Of what lasting value will be the reading skills being taught? Students must acquire enough skill in recognizing words, deriving word meanings, comprehending sentences and paragraphs, selecting only the pertinent data, evaluating the authenticity of materials, and grasping implied ideas so that they are ready to continue to be effective readers in a world that abounds in reading materials that report staggering discoveries, discuss crucial social and political problems, contain suggestions that will improve professional and vocational skills and insights, and afford deep pleasure in reading best sellers and less popular materials of quality.

The modern citizen must of necessity turn to reading materials to maintain his perspective on the changing scene. In like manner a critical reader must be able to choose among the thousands of titles published each year those books and periodicals that satisfy his values and needs. Good readers will choose to read a particular book not because it is a current fad but because it contains authentic information or depicts people and places accurately and artistically. Discrimination and judgment in the choice of books mark the mature reader; it is such qualities that high school teachers should cultivate in their best students.

Materials for the reading program. Despite the frequent criticisms of the reading ability of our secondary school students, they are probably reading more than the average adult, simply because they are required to read. All or practically all of the nontechnical reading material produced for the public can be read by the high school student who possesses average reading skills for his grade level. Reading materials for the high school student do not have to be geared to less-than-adult reading level.

There is no dearth of suitable, interesting materials for the secondary reading program. Excellent publications for the remedial and developmental programs are available from virtually every textbook publisher. Teachers and students can work together to bring to school materials which are both interesting and suitable to the needs of the students; much that the student enjoys on television and radio and in motion pictures can be related to his schoolwork and point the way to related reading. Students should be encouraged to subscribe to magazines and newspapers that contain materials of current importance related to their schoolwork. The teacher has an opportunity, through current materials, to help students develop a research point of view and follow research procedures that may continue as lifelong interests.

Summary

Careful planning by the administrative and teaching staffs is necessary for the successful initiation of a reading program in the secondary school. Problems that most often occur are:

1. A plan to involve all teachers in the program
2. Time to do the planning and the actual teaching of reading skills

3. Communication of the objectives of the program to students, to fellow teachers, and to parents
4. Selection of personnel to plan the reading program and to give in-service instruction to teachers who wish to participate in the program.
5. Adequate materials, in terms of both interest and ability levels.

Unless the program is carefully and thoughtfully planned to meet these problems and to provide instruction for both the reluctant and the superior student, it may be less than successful.

Suggested Readings

BOND, GEORGE W. "A Program for Improving Reading in the Secondary Schools," *School Review*, LX (September, 1952), 338–42.

EARLY, MARGARET J. "What Does Research Reveal about Successful Reading Programs?" *What We Know about High School Reading*. Champaign, Ill.; National Council of Teachers of English, 1957–58. Pp. 7–17.

FAY, LEO C. "The Developmental Program," *Reading in the High School: What Research Says to the Teacher*. Bulletin No. 11, National Education Association. Washington, D.C.: The Association, 1956. Pp. 13–31.

LEAMNSON, G. F. "Indianapolis Produces Better Readers," *School Executive*, LXXIV (December, 1954), 64–67.

Reading, Grades 7, 8, 9: A Teacher's Guide to Curriculum Planning. Curriculum Bulletin No. 11, 1957–58 Series. New York: Board of Education of the City of New York, 1959.

"Teaching Reading for the Gifted in the Secondary Schools," *Bulletin of the National Association of Secondary-School Principals*, XXXIX (October, 1955), 5–72.

The Suggestion Box

Using the check list given in the chapter, survey the local practices in the teaching of reading. Make a chart of the completed survey and use this as a basis of discussion with all staff members.

In each content area, use the check list of reading and study skills, and chart the results for that particular teaching area. Compare these composite charts from each content area.

Discuss with students in each course the demands which are made by teachers and content on the student's skills in reading. Does the information gathered from the students really aid the teacher in making more realistic assignments or in setting definite purposes for each assignment?

Discuss inter- and intraschool communication among elementary and secondary school teachers. How does improved communication provide better continuity in the teaching of reading and study skills?

Assign a group of class or faculty members to survey the local community for possible resource persons who could aid in the development of an improved reading program. Be sure to include in this survey outstanding elementary teachers and administrators, county and district consultants, college teachers, and other specialists.

IV

Interests and Preferences in the Reading of Adolescents

SINCE THE DEVELOPMENT OF A PERMANENT interest in reading is the ultimate goal of reading instruction, a program may be considered successful only as students turn voluntarily to books and periodicals for information and recreation. We may then hope that well-taught high school students will consider reading as important and fascinating an activity as attending a football game or watching a television program. This is especially likely to happen if reading is tied into their established interests and preferences.

What are the known interests of adolescents, and how well do we as teachers use these interests to give purpose and stimulation for reading and to aid in establishing in our students lifelong habits of reading? Do their choices of reading materials indicate that they have attained mature interests? Do they read worthwhile books? Do they turn voluntarily to reading as an adequate, satisfying means of using leisure time?

It is difficult to give definitive answers to these questions. Many studies and investigations have been made on the subject of reading interests and tastes of children and adolescents; not all have been carefully prepared nor analyzed to cover identical aspects of the reading habits of young people. Comparisons and conclusions are, therefore, difficult.

The interests of young people are as varied as the young people themselves. They are the product of many interrelated factors—intelligence, general maturity, home background, geographical location, past experience, cultural opportunities. These interests vary in kind, diversity, and intensity. Happily, they can be kindled, sustained, enriched, redirected, and heightened through skillful guidance.[1]

The results of a carefully planned and administered study were reported by George W. Norvell.[2] The goal of this study was to determine the differences in boys' and girls' reading interests and to use the results as a guide in selecting literary material for study in the secondary school. Seventeen hundred literary selections were tried out in all types of communities and all sizes of schools. More than 50,000 students and 625 teachers cooperated in the study.

Outcomes of the study were both interesting and significant. There were unmistakable implications for the reading program of secondary students. For example, it was clear

---

[1] John J. DeBoer, "The Changing Interests of Junior High School Students," *Reading in Action* (New York: Scholastic Magazines, 1957), p. 27.

[2] George W. Norvell, *The Reading Interests of Young People* (Boston: D. C. Heath and Co., 1950).

that worthwhile and classical literature ranks high in preferences of both boys and girls. Age, intelligence, and socioeconomic status apparently did not materially influence the likes and dislikes of students. Gifted and slow-learning pupils tended to state preferences for the same kinds of books; only the amount of reading appeared to differentiate the bright students from the slow-learners. There also was evidence that easy selections were not better liked by slow students and more difficult selections better liked by superior students. In other words, *content* and not *reading difficulty* is a major determinant of reading interests.

On the other hand, sex differences in choice of material were so marked that to overlook these differences would seem to endanger, if not prevent, the enjoyment of selections by a sizable number of students. Boys liked novels, plays, short stories, and biographies if the themes comprised adventure, outdoor life, mystery, obvious humor, sports, animals, patriotism, and men and boy characters. Girls liked all these, but they shunned grim adventure, war stories, and animal stories if the element of violence was prominent. In addition to the preferences of the boys, girls enjoyed biographies of women, stories of home and family, and plots based on romance and other sentiments. Boys expressed a marked interest in science material and, if written in a popular style, they rated it higher than adventure stories.

Norvell's study was based on data collected during the 1940's. It therefore appeared desirable to check on reading interests of boys and girls currently attending secondary schools. Two studies, conducted by Ben Leafe [3] and C. T. M.

[3] Ben Leafe, A *Survey of Reading Interests and Habits of High School Students in the Sacramento Area* (Unpublished M. A. Thesis, Sacramento, Calif., State College, 1958).

Johnson [4] in 1958, generally support the findings that were earlier reported by Norvell. These studies were conducted in the metropolitan area of Sacramento, California. One thousand students in the seventh and eighth grades were surveyed by Johnson; one thousand students in grades nine through twelve were surveyed in the Leafe study. An interest inventory was personally administered by the investigators to all types of classes: English, social science, industrial arts, along with others. A copy of the inventory used for these studies is to be found in the appendix of this book.

Most significant of the findings in these studies are:

1. A large number of students do not read comic books regularly, but state preference for the "popular" periodicals: *Life, Look, Reader's Digest,* and *Saturday Evening Post.* The percentage of students who profess interest in comic books declines steadily through the upper grades.

2. Interest in reading the daily newspaper was expressed by nearly all of the students surveyed. The three most popular sections of the newspaper are the front page, the comics, and the sports page. Boys appear to be more interested in articles on science and sports, while girls seem to be interested primarily in stories of people and places.

3. Apparently a peak in the amount of reading done is reached during the junior high school years. A steady decline in the number of books read is reported throughout the upper grades of the high school.

4. Age and maturity appear to be factors in determining selectivity in reading. More general interests are expressed

---

[4] C. Tobias M. Johnson, *A Study of the Reading Interests of Seventh and Eighth Grade Pupils in the Arden-Carmichael Union School District of Sacramento County, California* (Unpublished M. A. Thesis, Sacramento State College, 1958).

by seventh and eighth graders; more definite, narrowed interests are reported by eleventh and twelfth graders.

5. There do not appear to be significant differences in the types of reading done by low-achievers as compared to superior-achievers. This conclusion is drawn from the information gained by studying homogeneous groupings in both elementary and secondary schools.

6. Most of the students asserted that they selected their own books. An overwhelming majority of the students in both the elementary schools and the secondary schools denied that the teacher had influenced their choices. They also reported that parents or librarians had wielded little influence on their choices.

7. Common interests of both boys and girls, throughout the span of grades surveyed, are careers, adventure, biography, and science fiction.

The interests of adolescents are perhaps best characterized by the changes that occur with maturity, in terms of both the individual and the group. We have much evidence that changes in interests occur in each succeeding generation, but perhaps the most significant finding of the studies which have been reported in this century is that a wide range of interests exists among youngsters of any age group. A comparison of the findings in the Leafe and Johnson studies, in terms of types of books preferred, indicates rather clearly the changes that occur with maturity. See the summary lists that follow:

Analysis of these lists indicates a need for a wide variety of reading material for young people. Do they imply that the school should make a critical appraisal of practices con-

Preferences of Types of Books as Expressed by Two Thousand Boys and Girls, Grades Seven through Twelve

Seventh and Eighth Grades

Girls	Boys
1. Mystery	1. Science Fiction
2. Romance	2. Mystery
3. Animals	3. History
4. Religion	4. Biography
5. Biography	5. Animals
6. Classical Fiction	6. Sports
7. Travel and Exploration	7. Travel and Exploration
8. Science Fiction	8. Technical
9. Careers	9. Careers
10. History	10. Classical Fiction

Ninth through Twelfth Grades

Girls	Boys
1. Romance	1. Sports
2. Mystery	2. Science Fiction
3. Classical Fiction	3. Mystery
4. History	4. Classical Fiction
5. Travel and Exploration	5. History
6. Biography	6. Travel and Exploration
7. Careers	7. Technical
8. Religion	8. Biography
9. Science Fiction	9. Animals
10. Animals	10. Careers

nected with the study of literature? It is probable that rigid requirements of book lists and ways of reporting are liable to exert a negative influence on reading. If parents and teachers fail to provide sufficient variety in reading matter, they cannot expect pupils to find reading a consistently pleasurable experience. They must ask themselves: What resources and techniques can be utilized to guide the reading of adolescents to new heights?

A "revolution" has occurred during the past decade in publication, with the advent of standard classics in paperback form; never before has so much good reading been available to the general public for such a small investment. How can teachers utilize this source of materials to aid students in the development of broader interests, particularly in communities where library facilities are limited but specifically in all secondary classes which now depend exclusively on the use of a textbook or anthology?

The needs of adolescents. Havighurst, in his book *Developmental Tasks and Education,* has defined four tasks which are important for the adolescent:

1. Acquiring emotional independence of parents and other adults
2. Achieving assurance of economic independence
3. Selecting and preparing for an occupation
4. Desiring and achieving socially responsible behavior.[5]

This author further points out that successful achievement of a developmental task leads to the happiness and success of the individual; but failure to achieve the task leads to unhappiness, difficulty in making later adjustments, and some disapproval by peers and by society as a whole. Interests naturally cluster around the individual's concerns about himself and his relationships with other people, especially his peers. Young people, particularly secondary school students who

[5] See Robert J. Havighurst, *Developmental Tasks and Education* (New York: Longmans, Green and Co., 1954), chap. 5.

are at all stages of the turmoil of adolescence, are attempting
to come to terms both with their life at the moment and with
the adulthood which is imminent. They feel real needs to
live more fully than the limits of direct experience make
possible; consequently, they seek knowledge and vicarious
experience beyond themselves and their immediate environment. They seek answers to questions which arise as a result
of everyday changes in their physical, emotional, social, and
intellectual development.

The real job is not so much to *meet* as it is to *direct* and *channel*
reading interests, and to do this, we must get "down deep be-
neath" where adolescents—and children and adults—really live to
discover the wellsprings from which interests derive and to select
for emphasis those interests which can provide important touch-
stones of a maturing mind and spirit.[6]

One might reasonably question a recent tendency among
educators and librarians to brand as "undesirable" certain
classics, familiar folk tales, and short stories—undesirable
because they contain elements of violence, greed, and conflict. In coming to grips with life the young person seeks
through his reading solutions to many of his puzzling problems which arise in his relationships with people who are
both "evil" and "good." We have no evidence that the reading of *The Adventures of Tom Sawyer, Vanity Fair,* or
Hansel and Gretel has thrust a young person into a life of
crime and violence or that it has awakened undesirable
interests. The adolescent's interests in the fantastic, the bi-
zarre, the unrealistic are but an extension of his earlier de-

[6] Dwight L. Burton, "Developing a Reading Program That Will Meet
These Interests," *Reading in Action* (New York: Scholastic Magazines,
1957), p. 30.

light in the make-believe and "the stepping stone . . . to
the eternal awe of the unknown and the occult." [7]

Teachers have a serious responsibility for helping students
to face realistically many of the conflicts that arise in human
relations, and to help them develop discrimination in terms
of socially desirable and undesirable behavior. The world of
great literature is potentially a powerful teacher.

Helping students develop interests. Some pupils profess so
many diverse interests, pursue so avidly these varying interests in their reading, and move from one area to another
so rapidly that we have cause to be concerned whether they
will develop depth in any one area; others will report that
they are interested in only one narrow subject and will deny
the value of reading outside of that area. The restricted number who report no definite interests are likely to be the students who do not read well, who come from culturally
starved backgrounds, or who are reluctant to read because
of a fear of failure or fear of adult criticism. It is evident
that the interests of adolescents are marked by both change
and range. The teacher cannot hope to be able to satisfy all
the potential interests of youth, but he must help them
to develop and to explore as many of their interests as he
possibly can.

He can begin, perhaps, by assuming that most students
are interested in those things which refer to their basic needs
and aspirations: gaining knowledge about other people and
how they live, learning about and choosing a vocation, considering courtship and marriage and family life, developing
awareness of the commonality of human experiences, preparing for a college career, pursuing a hobby, sharing adven-

[7] *Ibid.*, p. 31.

tures, anticipating their roles as citizens in our society, and solving their personal problems. Such areas as these provide the teacher with successful bases for the selection of books and periodicals with which he can surround his students in his classroom.

It is not enough to suggest that students visit the library to select a book. Sometimes a job of "selling" students on the idea of reading is necessary. Why not, if we truly regard reading as an indispensable part of living? Certainly time should be set aside during the week for students to browse among a wide variety of books and periodicals. There should be periods of absolute freedom, during which students feel free to choose, to read, and to discuss books with each other and with their teacher. There should be periods in which readings are reported to the group as a whole. In such periods, criticism could be invited from other students regarding the accuracy of reading and reporting, the general effectiveness of presentation, and the value of the report to the group as a whole.

We should capitalize upon the students' interests in television and the movies by promoting the reading of books and articles which will not only intensify the pleasure in television or movie presentation but will also aid young people in setting standards for themselves with regard to the level of their listening and viewing.

Our guiding of reading interests takes on a most serious dimension when we realize that the great popular level of vicarious experience—represented by comic books, the pulps and slicks, and the great majority of radio, TV, and motion picture fare—panders to immaturity and presents a reconstruction of experience that is half true.[8]

[8] *Ibid.*, p. 31.

Teachers of all content areas should be aware of the teen-age books which can be used effectively to develop interest in a particular subject. We have a wealth of science fiction, biography, historical fiction, classical literature, and technical materials that can be used to expand knowledge and deepen understandings which textbooks introduce. So often the high school English teacher is the only one who considers the reading interests of the students; actually, some of the most interesting and provocative writing for young people has been done by social, physical, and natural scientists.

Finally, the teacher should seize every opportunity to discuss interests with students. Although an interest inventory may be a useful device, too often it will reflect what a pupil thinks his teacher prefers. For instance, a poll of the interests of boys and girls in the high school at the present time may indicate a high preference for science fiction or professional treatises on the world of science. The moot question is whether responses of students in today's high school represent *true* interests or whether they reflect the current emphasis upon science and mathematics as worthwhile endeavors of young people; also, may such responses reflect not interests but youth's realization that proficiency in science and mathematics is becoming increasingly emphasized for college admission? Class discussions, club meetings, extracurricular events, and social activities provide wonderful opportunities for teachers to listen to and gather clues regarding the current interests of their students. It is in such situations that students "lower their guards" and speak freely of themselves, their hopes, their aspirations, their prejudices, and their problems. It is a wise teacher who will use his eyes and ears as means of collecting clues, and then will gently lead the student to a book.

Summary

Studies of the interests of students in the secondary school indicate that intelligence and socioeconomic status are not the most crucial factors in the selection of reading materials; the most important factor appears to be the divergent interests of the two sexes at various age levels.

Junior high school students are apparently reading in larger amounts and with a wider range of interests than are senior high school students. However, the former are probably less discriminating and confirmed, since their choices waver between the interests of the intermediate-grade pupil and the adult. Both boys and girls indicate the importance of action and pace in the books they read.

Most students in the secondary school deny the influence of parents, teachers, or librarians in their choice of reading materials. Television and movie versions of books and plays apparently do provide motivation for reading the original versions.

To aid the student in developing worthwhile and lasting interests, the teacher must recognize the basic needs of the particular age group in regard to their emotional, social, intellectual, and physical development; he should then attempt to help adolescents solve their own problems through reading. The fostering of worthwhile interests in young people is the responsibility of every teacher of every subject in the curriculum.

Suggested Readings

BURTON, DWIGHT L. "Campaigning to Get Students to Read," *Bulletin of the National Association of Secondary-School Principals,* XXXIX (September, 1955), 34–43.

DEBOER, JOHN J. "What Does Research Reveal about Reading and the High School Student?" *What We Know about High School Reading.* Champaign, Ill.: National Council of Teachers of English, 1957–58. Pp. 35–45.

NORVELL, GEORGE W. *The Reading Interests of Young People,* Boston: D. C. Heath and Co., 1950.

SMITH, DORA V. "Guiding Individual Reading," *Reading in the High School and College.* 47th Yearbook, National Society for the Study of Education. Chicago: University of Chicago Press, 1948. Pp. 180–205.

WITTY, PAUL. "Reading Interests and Habits of Students," *Reading in the High School and College.* 47th Yearbook, National Society for the Study of Education. Chicago: University of Chicago Press, 1948. Pp. 19–24.

The Suggestion Box

Check course outlines in content areas and compare the required or suggested readings with the findings of Norvell, Leafe, and Johnson (cited in this chapter).

Survey carefully the anthologies which are used in the English program to determine the balance between "contemporary" and "classical" selections. From the teacher's experiences, what has been determined regarding the students' interests in the various selections?

Pose this question with members of a class: If I (the teacher) could use only five selections from those which we have studied this year, which five should I use in future classes?

As a substitute for the traditional book report, announce a competition among the students in "selling" a book to other members of the class, with the intention of awakening interest in a particular title. The presentation should be judged on the basis of speech qualities, organization of ideas, and soundness and effectiveness of presentation. Evaluation of the student's efforts should be on the basis of the interest aroused in his classmates.

Compile a list, for reluctant readers, of books which contain adult characters and activities but which are written at a simple level. Example: *Deep Sea Adventures*, published by Harr-Wagner.

Distribute study guides for films and television productions. Follow up with discussions and attempt to get an estimate of the number of students who have been sufficiently stimulated to read the book.

V

Identifying Problem Areas

A SERIOUS AND DIFFICULT PROBLEM INVOLVED IN setting up a secondary school reading program is that of evaluation, partially because the term means so many different things to different people. To some it means simply the administration of tests to secure an achievement score, which will be used as a basis for assigning students to certain English classes. To others the term connotes a diagnostic approach: just what skills are developed, which are lacking, and in what areas should help be given first? To still another group, evaluation is subjective—the worth of a particular technique or facet of a program, as reflected in the satisfactions of both teacher and pupils. Evaluation is all of these, and much more, for the purposes of evaluation are manifold:

1. To assess the needs of students in terms of current curriculum practices in all content areas
2. To determine the nature of instruction in order to meet the goals of the individual content areas
3. To determine the level of reading competency in order to

predict a student's success in reading at more advanced levels

4. To test the effectiveness of developmental and corrective instruction
5. To determine the need for special materials or for more appropriate materials for the content area
6. To aid in the personal and vocational guidance of students
7. To assess the values and possible deficiencies of the specific reading materials that are available.

Hundreds of thousands of tests, both achievement and special aptitude tests, are given each year to hundreds of thousands of students throughout the secondary schools of our nation. One cannot for a moment deny the value of a broad testing program when the results are used to determine achievement levels of the students and to set goals for the curriculum. However, too often the results of the testing program are unknown to the people who need them most— the classroom teachers. Test results are not solely the province of the guidance specialist or the administrator; they must, if effective evaluation is to be achieved, be disseminated to every teacher who is participating in the education of individual students who have been tested. An adequate testing program is the heart of evaluation in the school, but to be really effective the results of testing must be used by the teacher who has daily contact with the student.

A full program of appraisal will include not only (1) standardized tests, but (2) teacher-made tests and questionnaires, (3) informal observations, (4) permanent records, and (5) personal interviews. The teacher plays the most important role in the identification of superior and retarded readers. The standardized test gives the first indication of the achievement of the student; but the day-by-day observations of the teacher, as the students attempt to read in science, social studies, English, and a half dozen other subjects, give specific information which should be used to supplement test results. The information gained from a thorough appraisal can then be used to set up a corrective program for those students who need additional help and a developmental program for those who must be prepared to use the advanced skills which are demanded by the increasingly complex subjects.

Despite the soundness of our instructional procedures, we all too often fail to reach a large number of students who need help in the reading skills demanded in a particular content area. Some students have even been assigned to reading improvement classes with little or no regard for their willingness to put forth the effort demanded for improvement, little understanding of their capacity for improvement, and virtually no regard for individual interests. Also, instructional procedures which have been used successfully with one group of students may result in failure for another group. We cannot assume, at any time, that instruction can remain static. Some students will succeed in spite of rigidities and lack of scope in a reading program, but many will fail. Need we not, then, evaluate instructional procedures to determine why so many fail?

Obviously it is unfair to teacher and students alike if there is a lack of information about students who are participating in a reading improvement program. We have arrived at a point in education where we no longer believe in a single approach to teaching; still, to assume that a group of students need an emphasis upon certain skills, simply because it has been found that some students need those skills, is to overlook the wide range of individual differences which we know exist in each new group of students. New needs are constantly being identified, and our program of instruction must be adapted to meet them. For instance, teachers of reading improvement courses have found that their students often have difficulty with word-recognition skills. To offer a mass of easy reading materials to those students under the assumption that wide reading will improve *all* skills may result in a tragic waste of time for both students and teacher and eventual failure of the entire program.

No standardized test has been designed which will identify all the specific needs of the student for reading skills development, nor do the producers of standardized tests claim that their products will do an all-inclusive job. Many times the need of the student is one which is felt only by him; for example, the boy who reports that he desires to read better in order to enjoy his favorite hot-rod magazine—a perfectly legitimate desire of a typical teen-age boy. Even so, all the information we can gather on this student is going to be of value in setting up a program which will meet his immediate needs and fulfill long-range goals which we, as teachers, would feel are more important than the immediate goal of reading a hot-rod magazine.

The administrator or teacher might argue that there is not time for an elaborate appraisal program, since the instructional program demands all the time of the teacher. It is appropriate to point out that hundreds of man-hours of instruction are wasted each year on students whose needs have not been adequately identified; the goals of education are best met by spending as much time as necessary on accurate appraisal of needs and appraisal of the effectiveness of instruction.

Let us examine the various means of evaluating the progress of students in order that a sound reading program, in all content areas, may be initiated.

Standardized Tests

As we have indicated, most secondary schools have a program of evaluation based on standardized tests. How do we select appropriate tests for determining the needs of students in the reading area? These are the criteria to keep in mind:

1. Does the test really measure that which it purports to measure? Is it a test of reading, or does it sample a very narrow range of the total reading tasks with which the student is concerned? In other words, is the content of the test representative of materials from English, social science, science, and other content areas?
2. Do the results give a broad picture of the student's reading ability, or do they merely define ability to react silently to reading matter? Is the student required to skim, to organize ideas, to react to ideas, to select relevant details, to make decisions on the basis of facts or opinions presented, and to interpret what he has read in light of his personal experience and previous knowledge?
3. Can the test be administered with a minimum of effort and frustration? (Length of a test is not necessarily a criterion of validity, but a valid test must sample adequately. The argument for a test which can be administered during one period of the school day should be discarded if it can be shown that the test which requires two or three periods for administration actually gets at desired information.)

4. Can the results of the test be made meaningful to both the student and the teacher? In other words, do the results yield some indication of areas which need to be emphasized in the instructional program, in addition to informing the student of his relative standing with reference to norms?

5. Is the test reliable? (A popular means of evaluating the effectiveness of instruction is through the test-retest technique, in which the student is given a test at the beginning of a period of instruction and a parallel form of the same test at the end of the period of instruction. A test which has been carefully standardized should yield reliable results. On the other hand, the effectiveness of instruction should not be judged solely on the basis of test results; factors of increased interest and attention, motivation, and effort cannot be appraised by the ordinary reading test.)

6. Does the test actually differentiate between the student who can profit from instruction and the student who is now working at his ability level? (There is no one test available which will give this much-desired information; still, this is one of the most critical areas of the program. The decision must be made as to which students are to be admitted to a developmental program, which ones need corrective reading, and still others who have such limitations that they really could not profit from further training. Decisions such as these appear to be almost impossible when we consider the great numbers of students we now have in our secondary schools.)

The selection of a good standardized test for the reading program is relatively simple if we do not expect the test to yield all the information we need. No single test will yield all the desired information, but many can be used in combination to cover more areas of the curriculum and to gain a more accurate appraisal of the various reading skills. A list of dependable tests follows:

Durost-Center Word Mastery Test, Grades 9–12

Two parts: (1) a measure of general vocabulary level of secondary school students and (2) a measure of the student's ability to learn the meanings of unknown words by seeing them in typical contexts.

Total time: 60 minutes

World Book Company

Gates Reading Diagnostic Tests, Revised Edition, Grades 1–8. A long test, the Gates Diagnostic yields measures of important areas of reading: oral reading, speed of reading paragraphs, vocabulary, phrase perception, word perception and analysis, spelling, visual perception, and auditory discrimination. It is designed to be used with the individual student to discover specific disabilities.

Forms: I, II

Total time: about 75 minutes

Bureau of Publications, Teachers College, Columbia University

Gilmore Oral Reading Test, Grades 1–8

A series of oral reading paragraphs, designed to be a diagnostic instrument to discover specific disabilities. This is one of the best tests on the present-day market and can be used to assess quickly the errors which the student habitually makes while reading.

Forms: A, B

Total time: unlimited

World Book Company

Iowa Every Pupil Tests of Basic Skills: Silent Reading Comprehension, Advanced Battery, Grades 5–9

This test yields three scores: vocabulary, reading comprehension, and total. It will be noted that this test is most useful in the junior high school, but it has been used successfully with all levels of retarded readers in the high school, who typically read several levels below their grade placement.

Forms: L, M, N, O

Total time: 68 minutes
Houghton Mifflin Company

Iowa Every Pupil Tests of Basic Skills: Work Study Skills, Grades 5–9
Five parts: map reading, use of references, use of the index, use of the dictionary, and reading graphs, charts, and tables.
Forms: L, M, N, O
Total time: 77 minutes
Houghton Mifflin Company

Kelley-Greene Reading Comprehension Test, Grades 9–12
Three parts: paragraph comprehension, directed reading, and retention of details. Rate of reading also may be estimated.
Forms: Am, Bm, Cm
Total time: Test 1, 20 minutes; Test 2, 33 minutes; Test 3, 10 minutes
World Book Company

Michigan Vocabulary Profile Test, High School and College
Tests the student's knowledge of words generally used in eight areas: commerce, government, physical science, biological science, mathematics, fine arts, and sports. 240 items, based on a four-choice system.
Forms: Two equivalent forms
Total time: unlimited, but usually requires about one hour
World Book Company

Reading Comprehension: Cooperative English Test, Lower Level, C–1, Grades 7–12
Four scores: vocabulary, speed of comprehension, level of comprehension, and total. A good screening test for determining those students who lack general reading ability.
Forms: R, S, T, Y
Total time: 40 minutes
Educational Testing Service

School and College Ability Tests, Grades 4–14
Excellent for determining the student's capacity for learning.

Three scores: verbal, quantitative, and total
Forms: four levels, 4 forms at each level
Educational Testing Service

Sequential Tests of Educational Progress, Grades 4–14
Measures achievement in seven areas: reading, writing, science, mathematics, social studies, listening, and essay writing.
Forms: 4 levels, 2 forms at each level
Educational Testing Service

Stanford Achievement Tests: Advanced Reading, Grades 7–9
Two parts: word meaning and paragraph meaning. Exercises are designed to measure not merely the simpler functions of recognition or word matching but also higher-level comprehension and inference.
Forms: J, K, L, M, N
Total time: 37 minutes
World Book Company

The combination of an oral reading test with a silent reading test is desirable. While the silent reading test gives the teacher or counselor an indication of the level of achievement of the student, the oral reading test is needed to indicate the errors or patterns of errors consistently made by the student in word-recognition skills, phrasing, observing punctuation, and the like. The teacher will be interested to find the discrepancy that often exists between the student's silent and oral readings. For the remediation of disabilities, knowledge of specific reading skills is necessary. Such knowledge is hidden in the achievement scores of a silent reading test. When students have been grouped on the basis of a silent reading test, further testing with oral reading tests should indicate instructional procedures.

The combination of an intelligence test with a reading test

is also seriously recommended. Too often decisions are made
for students on the basis of their performance on a silent
reading test, with no regard for their ability levels. Occasionally a student's reading achievement will exceed that level
which we might have predicted for him on the basis of an
intelligence test; this student is generally highly motivated
and has developed his skills through great effort and concentration. On the other hand, a highly intelligent student
who is achieving at a level far below his capacity for learning might be seriously misjudged if we were to depend solely
on the results of the achievement test.

Results of standardized tests should be kept in a file that
is available to every teacher and is summarized in such a
manner that the teacher can interpret them without having
to consult each test folder. Teachers frequently have need
to verify their observations of students in the classroom,
and test results can be of real value in such cases.

The administration, scoring, and reporting of standardized
tests should be under the direction of a trained psychometrist
or psychologist, who serves as the testing officer for the
school or the district. This person should be available for con-
sultations with teachers when problems arise regarding the
progress of individual students. Individual testing of the diagnostic type should be done by the teacher; however, if he
is not qualified to give individual tests, he should be free to
call upon the testing officer for help. Tests such as the *Gilmore Oral Reading Test* are easy to administer and to score;
and to be really effective they should be administered
by the teacher who then uses the results to plan his instructional procedures for the particular student or group of
students.

Teacher-made Tests

The teacher plays the major role in identifying the student who needs help with his reading difficulties. Where standardized tests may fail to indicate areas of specific skills development or retardation, the teacher-made test can yield valuable information. Several techniques have been used by teachers in constructing these incidental tests.

One method could be the assignment of a number of pages in a particular textbook for rapid reading. These steps should be followed: Make a word count on the material covered, and determine the words per minute read by each student. Follow the reading exercise with good comprehension questions, constructed to determine:

1. knowledge of stated facts
2. knowledge of author's opinions
3. ability to infer meaning implied by the author
4. ability to identify the central idea
5. ability to recognize supporting details
6. knowledge of word meanings in the particular context
7. ability to read and follow directions.

Of course, constructing such a test is not easy, nor is it implied that each teacher-made test should emphasize all these criteria. But it is important that the teacher have a specific purpose when he constructs a test and that he devises a test consistent with that purpose. A single criterion or a combination of the criteria for a particular reading selection will point to definite expected outcomes.

Another factor to be considered in the teacher-made test is the type of reading material to be used. The English teacher may be interested in learning how well his students read magazine articles as contrasted with study materials. He will then provide opportunities for reading newspaper editorials, sports articles, a short story from a periodical, a factual biography, and many other types of materials. If a narrow range of reading abilities is demonstrated by a particular student, he lacks flexibility and consequently needs instruction in the adjustment of rate of reading to the purpose for reading and the content of the material.

A third factor in teacher testing is the determination of the instructional levels for each student. Each student has four levels of reading competency:

1. The instructional or teaching level—that level at which the student is capable of reading and receiving ideas with the aid of instruction.
2. The independent level—that level at which the student is capable of reading independently.
3. The frustration level—that level at which the student is no longer capable of reading the material and receiving the ideas.
4. The hearing comprehension level—the highest level at which the student is capable of receiving ideas as he listens.

Each level of competency is dependent upon the student's capacity to learn as well as his reading ability. A wide discrepancy between the hearing comprehension level and the actual reading level of the student generally indicates the degree of retardation.

The value of the teacher-made test lies in its use as a means of assessing the student's immediate needs in terms of a particular assignment, a unit of work, or an entire course. If these tests are constructed with care and with attention to particular criteria they may give the teacher valuable clues for determining the most effective instructional procedures.

Observations

In studying the needs of students, the teacher is in a position to observe daily certain factors which affect reading ability but are not measurable by a test. It is important that the teacher form the habit of writing down these observations which appear to reflect insight into the student's problems; it is futile to trust memory for the recall of pertinent data. Here are some examples of the types of observations which may have relevance to the reading problems of students:

1. The student who never finishes an assignment
2. The student who complains that assignments are too long
3. The student who frequently makes excuses for his lack of progress
4. The student who uses a pencil or his finger to guide his reading
5. The student who is unable to use reference materials
6. The student who exhibits poor work habits
7. The student who habitually withdraws from reading
8. The student who is apparently capable of responding to oral instruction or discussion but is frustrated when confronted by a reading assignment
9. The student who overcompensates for his lack of reading ability by the development of physical skills, dramatic ability, or performance in the fine arts.

It cannot be emphasized too strongly that daily observations are vital to the identification of specific problem areas. Many teachers have found that setting up a notebook, with a page labeled with the name of each student, provides a good means of recording observations. At a later date, if a case study is feasible, the teacher may find that the observation data, recorded at the time of the occurrence of the behavior, will shed light on the problem. Let us look at a typical case study which was initiated by a classroom teacher's observations:

Helen Larsen teaches English in the Walnut Hill High School. In one of her classes, an eleventh-grade American literature course, is Brian Blackwood, an outstanding basketball player and the son of a prominent Walnut Hill banker.

Brian is a handsome, well-developed young man who is one of the most popular students in the high school. He has been a student officer each year in the high school, and he is recognized as a leader in school activities.

About two months ago Miss Larsen gave her first assignment in her literature class—several poems by Poe. Brian objected loudly, stating that he didn't like poetry, and he especially didn't like Poe. Miss Larsen questioned him for a few minutes and discovered that Brian was bluffing; he actually didn't know who Edgar Allan Poe was. After class, Brian apologized to Miss Larsen, stating flippantly, "I guess I just wanted to give you a bad time."

On the following day, the class participated in reading poetry aloud, followed by discussion. Miss Larsen noted that Brian was quick to discuss, with real depth and insight, those poems which were read by other students. When Miss Larsen called on him to read his favorite, he rebelled, saying, "I told you yesterday that I didn't like Poe's poetry." When Miss Larsen remarked that Brian had done such a good job of discussing the poems which had been read by the other students, he replied, "Yes, but that was when someone else read."

Miss Larsen consulted Brian's cumulative record in the office of the principal and discovered several interesting and extremely revealing items. Brian Blackwood had consistently made C's in courses which required reading; in industrial arts, speech, and physical education, he had received all A's. Three teachers had made notation to the effect that Brian could not read well enough to keep up with the class, but that his ability to listen, to synthesize, and to discuss intelligently was well above average. A group intelligence test, administered when Brian was in the eighth grade, yielded a nonverbal intelligence score of 138; the verbal score was considerably lower—104. Achievement tests in arithmetic and the mechanics of language yielded scores above the 90th percentile; all reading scores were below the 20th percentile.

When Miss Larsen discussed Brian with his tenth-grade English teacher she learned that the teacher was doubtful about Brian's reading ability, but had always been impressed with his ability to lead discussions in the class.

A few days later Miss Larsen had an opportunity to talk with Brian after class. She asked him to remain for a few minutes, and she approached the matter of his reading cautiously. She was not prepared for the emotional outburst which followed. Brian was suddenly a little boy asking for help with a problem which had, for years, caused him shame and embarrassment. He related that at one time he could read as well as other members of his classes; he thought that perhaps he had no difficulty until about the fourth grade. "Then, one day," he related, "I realized I couldn't keep up with the rest of the class, but no one seemed to notice it except me. I couldn't finish my assignments, and my mother and my father started nagging at me because I didn't do my homework. That's when I started to be an athlete, and pretty soon I didn't seem to care much about the reading. Oh, I shouldn't say that I didn't care, because I did, and all the time I couldn't figure out why it was I seemed to be able to hold my own with the other kids in everything except reading. When I was in the eighth grade, I suddenly decided that I had to do something about my reading, but I got discouraged because nothing I did seemed to help. My high school teachers haven't said a word to me about my reading, but I've felt all along that they knew I couldn't read well. Miss Larsen, I want to go to college, but I'll never make it this way."

Miss Larsen recognized in Brian Blackwood two requisites for improvement—a keen mind and grim determination. Since that day of discussion with Brian she has worked with him one-half hour a day, three times a week, helping him to discover his weaknesses in skills and to strengthen those skills. On two occasions she has overheard Brian discussing his reading problems with other students, and she has been pleased with his objectivity and his honesty. Yesterday Brian Blackwood read aloud in English 11. His performance was not perfect, but he had prepared carefully for this occasion. Miss Larsen was surprised when he volunteered; she was thrilled when he had finished. He had read with sincerity, and he had chuckled twice at his own mistakes.

In addition to observing the problem areas of the students the teacher has a firsthand knowledge of the progress of each student, as demonstrated by his daily behavior. Any record of a student's progress should include indications of his *growth* in effective study habits, reading habits, and general academic achievement.

Cumulative Records

The cumulative record or permanent record card of the student often yields information which cannot be obtained elsewhere. To set up a program in reading for a particular student, the teacher would want to know:

1. His past academic record. In what subjects has he succeeded, failed? Is there indication of a time at which the student succeeded very well? When did he begin to fail, and did certain content subjects present difficulties which contributed to his failure?
2. The number of schools he has attended. Has this student moved often? Is there evidence of a lack of continuity in his academic training? Has his schooling been interrupted often, and for what reason? (Today's schools are filled with children of transient families: members of the armed forces,

engineers, and government officials. These are not the lower economic group which we ordinarily assume the transient to be. Their problems are those of interruption of training, lack of continuity, and conflicting educational systems.)

3. His health status. What evidence is there of visual and auditory acuity? Is there any history of physical or mental illness over a prolonged period of time?

4. His previous testing record. Is there evidence of his intellectual capacity? Have achievement scores shown rather consistent patterns or are there discrepancies in his performance?

5. His family background. What is the father's occupation? What is the marital status of the parents? Does the mother work? What language is spoken in the home? What evidence is there of parental interest or pressures? Is there a record of the academic performance of brothers and sisters? Are the parents well educated?

6. Previous history of special counseling or teaching. Some students become professional "shoppers" for the attention and time of counselors, administrators, and teachers. Is there evidence that the student has not responded favorably to previous attempts to give him help?

Very often cumulative records fail to give the desired information, since many high schools do not have records of the student's elementary school experiences. On the other hand, if the teacher is seeking means of judging the student's status and the possibilities of giving special instruction, any information relative to that student's past performance should be helpful.

Interview

If the teacher is to work on a program of skills development with a student, the personal interview can often be the most revealing source of information. This can be either structured, in which definite questions are posed by the teacher, or it can be totally unstructured. In the case of the student who is having difficulty, it is important for the teacher to know the following:

1. How does the student feel about his problem: what does he feel his problem is? What caused his reading difficulty? When did he first become aware of the difficulty?
2. What evidence is there of a lack of reading experience in the student's home and school background?
3. What are the student's interests, goals, aspirations? Does he have overpowering interests-of-the-moment which actually interfere with his schoolwork?
4. Is there any evidence of a lack of motivation to do better work? Has he adopted the "what's the use" attitude which is typical, for instance, of the underprivileged child of the migrant worker?
5. Is the student willing to assume responsibility for improving his skills or correcting his deficiencies?
6. Does he express any *need* for learning to read better? What values does he see in being able to read? Does he feel that his future lifework will demand reading skill?
7. How does he feel about his family? his peers? school?

A student-teacher relationship is often solidified by the opportunity for "talking things out." No improvement is going to be made by the boy or girl who feels that the teacher is there to force learning upon the group, nor can improvement be expected if the individual feels that the teacher is responsible for giving a panacea for academic difficulties. The student must be able to identify his own problems and with the aid of the teacher chart a course of skills development which he, himself, will assume responsibility for following. It is most important that the teacher recognize the student's own estimate of his improvement. It is often surprising to the teacher to discover that the student who has made no measurable progress, has, nevertheless, gained confidence in and respect for himself as a result of very slight improvement.

Summary

No program of evaluation is perfect, nor can it ever become perfected. We are constantly confronted with unknown quantities and qualities which cannot be fully assessed; but no program of reading instruction can be really meaningful unless evaluation is an integral part of that program.

The teacher cannot assume full responsibility for evaluating the needs of his students or the effectiveness of his instructional procedures. Trained technicians are needed to assist with the standardized testing program, both in terms of administration and interpretation of the results. If test results are available to the teacher, they may be used advantageously to determine the grouping of students for the most effective instruction; they should also reveal those areas of basic skills which need further emphasis. They should tell the teacher that many students are capable of reading widely and deeply; for these students, both acceleration and depth are indicated.

In addition to the information which may be obtained from tests, the teacher may prepare his own informal tests and questionnaires; he may record daily observations of the performance of his students as they encounter a variety of reading tasks. Occasionally he may, with the help of an administrator or a testing officer, wish to study and discuss the cumulative records which are kept on each student. Certainly he will take advantage of every opportunity to interview his students to determine their interests, their feelings about their progress in his particular subject, and their personal needs for improvement.

The purposes and goals of instruction are constantly changing; some of these changes are subtle and others are obvious. They will continue to change as we discover new means of determining the effectiveness of our present practices in education.

Good evaluation is determined, in part, by these criteria:

1. It is continuous, through the academic career of the student or a period of time covered by a particular course of study.
2. It is based not only on the in-school but also on the current and future out-of-school needs and goals of our young citizens.
3. It is broad in scope, embracing all the techniques which we now recognize as being helpful.

Suggested Readings

ARONOW, MIRIAM S., and WRIGHTSTONE, J. WAYNE. *The Informal Appraisal of Reading Abilities.* Educational Research Bulletin No. 10. New York: Board of Education of the City of New York, 1949.

BOND, GUY L. "Identifying the Reading Attainments and Needs of Students," *Reading in the High School and College.* 47th Yearbook, National Society for the Study of Education. Chicago: University of Chicago Press, 1948. Pp. 69–90.

MECKEL, HENRY C. "Evaluating Growth in Reading," *Reading in the High School and College.* 47th Yearbook, National Society for the Study of Education. Chicago: University of Chicago Press, 1948. Pp. 252–75.

NEWTON, EUNICE S. "Empirical Differences between Adequate and Retarded Readers," *The Reading Teacher,* XIII (October, 1959), 40–44.

ROBINSON, HELEN M. (comp. and ed.). *Evaluation of Reading.* Supplementary Educational Monographs, No. 88. Chicago: University of Chicago Press, 1958.

The Suggestion Box

Select identical achievement scores in reading for five students. Analyze the subtests of the test to determine, if possible, areas of strength and weakness for each student. Compare the achievement scores with past academic achievement of these particular students, particularly in those areas which have required broad reading. Determine, if possible, the intellectual capacity and general background of each student. These data should present interesting discrepancies. Discuss these students in a staff meeting to emphasize the need for careful evaluation.

Obtain a copy of Tinkelman's *Making the Classroom Test* from the New York State Education Department, Division of Tests and Measurements, Albany, N.Y. Use this as a basis for discussing staff problems in the preparation of teacher-made tests.

Observe carefully the reading and study skills of five selected students. Record daily behavior of these students as they work together and individually in reading situations. Interview these students to attempt to get insight into their problems and their particular techniques. If several teachers select the same five students, the data can be compared and contrasted in a case-study presentation for the teaching staff. Refer to the case study of Brian in this chapter.

Invite the school counselors to discuss with the teaching staff the problems of identifying reading levels of students as they relate to assignment of students to class sections. How can teacher judgments assist the counselors in making valid decisions?

Involve teacher groups in the selection and evaluation of tests for the different content areas.

VI

Basic Reading Skills

READING AT ANY LEVEL INVOLVES A FINE integration of a number of complex skills. Many students reach the secondary school with a background of systematic, sequential reading experiences and are ready for refinement, extension, and application of reading skills. Unfortunately, others may lack one or more essential skills and find themselves handicapped in meeting the demands of the secondary school. If it were possible to measure accurately the developmental levels of the various skills which various students present as they enter the secondary school, we would discover all stages of refinement.

It [reading] is . . . the process of interrelating many varied experiences, drawing meanings from these and associating these meanings with symbols that are almost infinitely varied in their combinations and permutations. It is, therefore, not a simple process that is mastered once and for all. As the student moves into the organized bodies of knowledge with their own technical terminologies and special vocabularies, in short their languages, he must to a degree learn to read again. Each special field has its own language and one who would succeed in the field must learn its language.[1]

The preceding paragraph makes evident the soundness of a planned, sequential secondary school reading program. The amount and complexity of material that the student must read, the specialized vocabularies, and the number of basic concepts in each subject area call for continued instruction in reading throughout the secondary school.

In planning such a reading program, a survey to determine group and individual needs is the initial step. Teachers should not be surprised to discover that even among superior groups mastery of skills is uneven. Some pupils may have limitations in vocabulary; others may have inadequate word-attack skills; many may read all types of material in the same manner and at the same speed; some may lack essential comprehension skills. Ascertaining the reading background for purposes of planning a developmental program in the individual classroom may appear to be time consuming; however, the reward will be found in the increased possibilities of developing a truly worthwhile reading program.

Methods of determining needs of the group and of individuals are developed in Chapter V, "Identifying Problem Areas." Informal tests, observations, questionnaires, interest inventories, records in cumulative folders, class discussions, and standardized tests will all contribute information upon which to base a reading program. The survey should help the teacher to determine:

[1] *What Shall the High Schools Teach?* (1956 Yearbook, Association for Supervision and Curriculum Development, Washington, D.C., p. 186.

1. The general ability of the group
2. Individual and group levels of achievement
3. Weaknesses in particular skills
4. The interests and attitudes of individuals
5. Amount and breadth of independent reading.

The type of program will vary according to the community, the budget of the school, the preparation of the teachers, and the goals that are set. All members of the faculty should participate in the program and should share outcomes with the total group.

In the secondary school, where different teachers teach different subjects and there is little effort made to coordinate assignments in the various subjects, the reading problem of the students can be a serious one. Some teachers ignore the need for pointing out to students what to look for, what important facts are to be selected, or how to read the material; they assume that these skills have already been developed by the students and, hence, need no further emphasis. Unless the student is a highly competent reader he may find it almost impossible to keep up with all the assignments; consequently, he may make the simple compromise of completing the assignment of the subject area in which he is interested and of inadequately preparing other assignments. This partially explains why a student may be doing outstanding work in science and almost failing work in social studies, for example.

What skills should the secondary school include in its reading program? Which skills are to be retaught, which are to be included in a maintenance program, and which are to be introduced for the first time?

Word-Recognition Skills

The extensive vocabulary in the various subject areas of the secondary school is often in striking contrast to the more limited vocabulary used in textbooks in the elementary grades. The most important tool in meeting this vocabulary load is the ability to figure out new words and to pronounce them. To check on the students' proficiency in this phase of reading, the teacher should use both oral and silent reading tests. His day-by-day observations of the difficulties experienced by students in attacking new words should give him valuable information concerning the skills to be taught.

Phonetic analysis. The recognition of symbols (single letters and letters in various combinations) and the sounds which they represent is known as phonetic analysis. Mastery and rapid recognition of numerous separate phonetic elements depend upon repetition and rote memory; consequently, phonetic analysis is extremely complex, particularly since the English language is phonetically irregular; for example, the same symbol may stand for more than one sound (phonemes):

a as in *hat;* a as in *rate;* a as in *wander;* a as in *about*

In the same manner, a phoneme may be represented by more than one symbol:

o—ow, ough, oa, oe, ou

Certain critics of reading practices in our schools have often stated that a return to the teaching of phonics would constitute a panacea for all reading ills. These critics are often uninformed as to the complexity and comparative unreliability of phonetics.

Some students need no formal instruction in phonetics; others could benefit greatly from a planned, sequential program directed at developing word-attack skills which are based on phonetic principles. The student who can attack new words readily understands the following procedures:

1. Hears and recognizes initial, final, and medial consonants.

   *m*ediocre (initial consonant)
   phanto*m* (final consonant)
   co*m*plete (medial consonant)

2. Hears and recognizes consonant blends

   *cr*awl (initial blend)
   poi*nt* (final blend)
   tri*nk*et (medial blend)

3. Hears and recognizes consonant digraphs

   *ch*astise (initial digraph)
   sear*ch* (final digraph)
   wor*sh*ip (medial digraph)

4. Hears and recognizes diphthongs

   b*oy*   c*ow*
   b*oi*l   m*ou*se

5. Hears and recognizes vowels

   a—h*a*t, w*a*de, c*a*re, c*a*r, *a*bout, r*a*w
   e—b*e*, m*e*t, wond*e*r, sl*ei*gh
   i—b*i*t, m*i*ce, b*i*rd, mar*i*ne
   o—l*o*ck, *o*ver, m*o*re, ab*o*ve, t*o*
   u—s*u*pper, m*u*se, c*u*rrent

A list of phonetic principles and examples of each can be found in Appendix D of this book. For a better understanding of phonetic analysis the teacher should read *On Their Own in Reading* by William S. Gray (Scott, Foresman and Co.) or secure handbooks which are prepared for teachers to accompany the basic reading series in the elementary grades. Excellent practice material for the student may be found in *Eye and Ear Fun,* Books 3 and 4 (Webster Publishing Co.), and *Phonics Skilltexts,* Books C and D (Charles E. Merrill Co.). Although these workbook manuals are written for use with elementary school students, they may be used effectively with the high school student who needs practice in the rapid recognition of words. If this type of practice material is used, particular care should be taken to ensure transfer of the skills to actual reading practice. As understanding and competency are evident in each category, attention should be shifted to the next level of difficulty, but maintenance of the skills should be ensured through frequent review of the various skills.

The sequence to be followed in the teaching of phonetic analysis is, of course, from the simple to the complex. The more general and universal applications should be mastered before any attempt is made to teach the less frequently used analytic skills. For example, single consonants in initial, medial, and final positions would be taught before considering blends and digraphs; long and short vowels would be taught before emphasizing double vowels and diphthongs.

Structural analysis. The analysis of the structural elements of words includes inflected forms, derived forms, compound words, and syllabication. Structural analysis may appear to be such an obvious type of word recognition that the teacher may minimize its importance; however, it is a highly important skill, since accurate pronunciation of new words often depends upon recognition of the structural elements. Many students can readily recognize a root word, but they fail to recognize that same word when an ending is added. For example, the word *like* may be recognized instantly, but the variant form *unlikely* is much more difficult if the student has not learned to scrutinize new words carefully for familiar elements. The prefix *un-* and the suffix *-ly* tend to conceal the presence of the root word.

Inflected forms indicate person, case, gender, number, tense, and comparison. The most common inflectional endings are *-s, -es, -ess, -er, -est, -en, -ed,* and *-ing.* The basic meaning of an inflected form is contained in the root word; consequently, attention should be directed to careful scrutiny of the word to determine the root word. Practice should be given in locating, pronouncing, and hearing the inflected forms. Special attention should be given to the principles which apply to the adding of endings; accurate spelling often depends on the knowledge of these principles. For example, when a monosyllable or a root word ends in a single consonant preceded by a vowel (*win*), the final consonant is doubled before adding the vowel ending: *winning.* In the case of a word with two or more syllables (*prefer*), the same rule applies if the accent is on the final syllable (*preferred*); otherwise, the final consonant is not doubled (*preference*). A list of the principles for adding inflectional endings is included in Appendix D.

The student who does not recognize inflected forms tends to omit the endings when he reads orally as, for example, pronouncing *asked* as if it were *ask.* To locate those students who need further practice in recognizing and pronouncing inflected forms the teacher should develop the habit of listening carefully as students read aloud. He should take notes on the types of endings that cause difficulty and the names of students who have this difficulty; direct instruction can then be given to any group of students who have a need in common.

Derived forms are those words which are combined with *prefixes* and *suffixes* (both referred to as *affixes*). Unlike the inflectional endings, prefixes and suffixes have meanings of their own, and when they are combined with a root form the meaning of the total form may be different. It is important to remember, however, that the meaning of the root form does not change: mature, *im*mature (not mature).

The analysis of derived forms, recognizing familiar elements in the word, is an excellent means of developing a meaning vocabulary. Russell Stauffer has done an analysis of common prefixes and lists fifteen which are most frequently used: [2]

ab-	— off from, away	— absent
be-	— completely	— bedecked
com-	— together with	— compress
de-	— down, from, away, out of	— detract
dis-	— apart from, reversing	— distract
en-	— in	— enamored
ex-	— out of, beyond, without	— exhale
in-	— into	— inhale
in-	— not	— inaccurate
pre-	— before	— predict
pro-	— forward	— protrude
re-	— back, again	— return
sub-	— under, secondary	— submarine
un-	— not	— uncommon

[2] Russell G. Stauffer, "A Study of Prefixes in the Thorndike List to Establish a List of Prefixes That Should Be Taught in the Elementary School," *Journal of Educational Research*, XXXV (February, 1942), pp. 453–58.

Two techniques which have been widely used by teachers to give practice in the recognition and understanding of derived forms are:

1. Select a root form and build a "family" of words, substituting and adding various prefixes and suffixes. Call attention to the fact that the meaning of the root form *does not change:*

voice	convocation
vocal	vocation
vocabulary	avocation
invoke	provoke
evoke	vociferous

2. Select a derived form and examine its components, calling attention to the meaning of each part. Ask the students to name other words which contain the components:

philosophy

*phil*anthropist	theo*sophy*
mis*anthropy*	pan*the*ism
*mis*ogamist	*Pan* American
bi*gamist*	anti-*American*
*bi*sect	*ant*agonist

Developing skill in the recognition of derived forms serves two purposes: expanding meaning vocabulary and gaining an understanding of the origin, or history, of words. An extensive list of prefixes, suffixes, and roots which are common in the English language has been included in Appendix D.

Compound words are those words which are a combination of two known words; neither word has changed meaning: *basketball, something, playground.* Students who do not recognize compounds have simply not learned to scrutinize words for familiar parts. It is important to stress also that neither word changes its spelling when the compound is formed; with this knowledge the student need not puzzle over the spelling of such a word as *bookkeeper* or *roommate*. Very few compound words are difficult, in either meaning or spelling.

Syllabication is the process of dividing words into pronunciation units, or syllables. An understanding of what constitutes a syllable is important; once the student knows that every syllable must contain a *vowel sound* he has at his command a method of breaking words into orderly divisions for the purposes of pronunciation. The associated skill of learning to pronounce words from glossaries and dictionaries should accompany any practice in syllabication. Hearing words pronounced and recognizing the number of divisions in the word is probably the first step; at the same time that the number of syllables is determined the student should be aware of the stress or accent on the various parts. This feeling for syllables and accent is closely related to musical patterns in detecting primary and secondary beats. Seeing the word divided, either by vertical lines or the short dash or dot, also is helpful in developing an awareness and understanding of syllables:

con-fis-ca-to-ry   or   con/fis/ca/to/ry

A list of principles which may be applied to syllabication is included in Appendix D of this book.

The *context clue* is an intelligent guess of the meaning of the word from its use in the sentence. Good readers depend more on context clues than any other recognition skill. If the context does not give a clue as to the meaning or pronunciation of the word, then the reader may resort to using phonetic, or structural, analysis of the word. There are several ways in which the author helps the reader with new words:

1. Inference: the reader's experience helps him to infer the meaning:
   The heat from our big fire came in and we were as warm as *toast.*
2. Direct explanation:
   The specialist on snakes, a *herpetologist,* showed us the poisonous and nonpoisonous snakes.
3. Use of an antonym:
   Everyone was to travel light; *excessive* weight of baggage would handicap the expedition.
4. Figures of speech:
   I watched with dismay as I observed in his face a rush of *volcanic* violence from which I had seen strong men withdraw.
5. Situation, attitude, tone, or mood of a particular writing:
   They at first thought that the snakes were wooden ones, and there was a noticeable *recoil* when they realized the reptiles were really alive.
6. Summary statement:
   Windows buckled and splintered, walls tottered and crumbled, a roof sagged weirdly, and a terrifying sheet of flame crept greedily upward and upward toward the adjacent walls of the convent; it was a *holocaust* unparalleled in my childhood experiences.

The ultimate goal in the teaching of word-attack skills is, of course, the ability to read fluently and efficiently without hesitating to ponder over new and unfamiliar words. The skilled reader may employ simultaneously two or more of the skills which we have discussed above; however, he seldom consciously attacks words, unless they are vague and lacking in any familiar elements. It is impossible to know exactly when a word moves from the stage of conscious, deliberate attack to the level of instant recognition; but the efficient reader is constantly adding to his sight vocabulary, which consists of those words which are instantly recognized without a conscious attack.

The teacher of reading must realize that the overuse of word-attack skills can be detrimental to fluency in reading. There is always a danger that the student will become so involved in the phonetic and structural analysis of words that he will develop into a mere "word-caller" who neglects the meaning of the word, the sentence, or the paragraph. Excessive separate drill on phonetic or structural analysis will result in bad habits that jeopardize the student's chances of becoming a really efficient reader. Practice on word-attack skills should always be directed toward the meaning of the words and the broader skills of comprehending the paragraph or the selection.

Vocabulary Skills

Pronouncing words is but one part of vocabulary work. One of the marks of an educated person is the breadth and depth of his meaning vocabulary. The adolescent should have acquired a sizable stock of words which will enable an exact statement of his views and, in turn, an accurate interpretation of what he hears and reads. Therefore, no opportunity should be overlooked to extend, enrich, and refine pupils' vocabularies. Direct and vicarious experiences should contribute to new insights, to modified meanings, and to subtle connotations of words.

Students need to be reminded that each unfamiliar word

need not be learned as an entirely new element. Rather, the
first procedure is to take a careful look at each new word
and see the relationship or similarity it may bear to words
already mastered, or to listening to the pronunciation of the
word in order to perceive familiar elements. Because words
heard in context are more readily interpreted and understood
than words encountered in reading matter, the students
should be guided to select terms from radio, television, films,
and discussions for inclusion in their present personal vocabulary. If the classroom is made a place where students may
share vocabulary interests, there will be abundant opportunity for all students to enrich and extend word knowledge.

Cumulative lists of words of personal interest to him should
be kept by each student. By the time students have reached
high school age most of them have some idea about future
plans. To begin the accumulation of words that will be useful
in a selected vocational field will make it possible to read
intelligently in the specialized area as well as to speak and
write clearly about it. The list should include the pronunciation, the meaning, and the use of the word in a sentence.

The *history,* or *etymology,* of words can be fascinating.
We are often told that the English language is an irregular
one, but how often do we hear explanations for these irreg-
ularities? Pupils will gain much if they are stimulated to seek
out answers to questions like these: What are the origins of
our language? Through what other languages have many
of our common words evolved to their present-day position
in English? A very helpful book, written for easy reading,
is *The Tree of Language,* by Helene and Charlton Laird

(World Publishing Co.). The authors give a succinct and highly interesting history of our language. A more difficult but extremely valuable book is Mario Pei's *Language for Everybody* (Pocket Books, Inc.). The handiest source of the history of any particular word is a good dictionary, either a desk or an unabridged edition.

Specific terms which are needed to describe a hobby, an experiment, a construction project, or a particular process are another area of interest to the student; he should be prepared to write unusual terms on the chalkboard and to repeat, if necessary, the meanings of the words. In this way the audience has an opportunity to learn new words. In a similar manner the teacher may introduce technical vocabulary which is necessary for clear understanding of a particular subject. Discussion of new words should be encouraged, and frequent opportunities should be created for the repetition of those words, either in writing or in speaking.

A knowledge of prefixes, suffixes, and roots which are common to many words in our language will simplify both pronunciation and meanings of words. No opportunity should be missed to discuss the meaning of a word that can be analyzed through application of this knowledge. In Appendix D is a list of common affixes and roots which the teacher and the student should find helpful in developing vocabulary skills.

The multiple meanings of words should receive specific attention in the classroom. Confused ideas and misinterpretations frequently occur when the student reads a word but fails to attach its proper meaning in a particular context. For example, note the ideas that are conveyed by the word *master* in each of the following illustrations:

The dog was faithful to his *master*.
He tried hard to *master* the technique of pitching.
The *master* copy has been destroyed.

In this same category of words are those which are spelled alike and pronounced similarly but have no relationship in terms of their meanings:

He received his just *desert* (due reward or punishment).
He was forced to *desert* the project (abandon or forsake).

On the other hand, words which are alike in spelling but different in pronunciation are often closely related in meaning:

The *deserted* house stood in the midst of a vast *desert*.

It is easy to assume that students understand such subtle differences among words, simply because many such words are simple to pronounce and are commonly used. That students do have difficulty with these words is evident, however, in discussions and in oral reading in the classroom.

The connotations of words are often strictly personal; words that carry feelings along with meaning need special discussion. Consider the word *retreat* in the following context:

What kind of *retreat* are you planning?

To the religious person, this may suggest a time of meditation and prayer; to the lover of isolation, it means a place away from the crowds; and to one who has experienced defeat, it may mean withdrawal. It is never safe to assume that emotionally flavored words convey the same idea to all individuals. *Words and What They Do to You* by Catherine Minteer (Row, Peterson and Co.) is a good book for the student who is seeking a basic knowledge of semantics.

Qualifying words and transitional words and phrases also should be included in the teaching of vocabulary skills. *Many, few, almost, every,* and *occasionally* are examples of words which may qualify the meanings of other words or phrases. *However, moreover, nevertheless, on the contrary,* and *hence* are examples of words which alert the reader to a shift in emphasis. The good reader will pay particular attention to words of this type, since he recognizes that such words are actually signaling him to be ready for a shift in meaning or emphasis.

Vocabulary building should receive constant emphasis in the classroom. The best example of breadth and depth in vocabulary should be the teacher, who chooses words for effectiveness and clarity, deliberately introduces new words into discussion, and each day calls attention to the variety and power of words.

Comprehension Skills

Most students will be functionally literate if they are able to interpret the plain sense or literal meaning of the material. The ability to get the directly stated facts should be the *minimum* expectation for secondary students. Who did it? When did it happen? Where did it happen? What happened first? next? last? are the types of questions that bring out the essential facts in a reading selection.

Main ideas. However, because masses of undifferentiated facts are not too useful, students should be taught to organize ideas under main thoughts and supporting details. Instruction and practice in applying this one skill will improve immeasurably a student's performance in all subject areas. Exercises such as finding the topic sentence, writing a suitable title or marginal heading, or phrasing a good question about the paragraph are some ways to focus the student's attention on "What was this about?"

Details. Students should understand the importance of *details* as they support and expand the main idea; details should not be seen as discrete facts. Moreover, they should learn to discriminate between the essential and the unimportant details. The following techniques will be found helpful:

1. An outline of three or four main ideas is placed on the chalkboard. Students discuss and attempt to agree on the details necessary to complete the outline.
2. A "treasure hunt" type of exercise is developed. Several topics are listed. Relevant and irrelevant clues are arranged under the list. The selection of the proper clues for each topic and the elimination of those that applied to none of the topics will test ability to select relevant details.
3. Topics relating to steps in a process, a sequence of events, or a series of comparisons are arranged under main idea and subheads.
4. Students are asked to read to discover the topic sentence in a paragraph or series of paragraphs. Next they are to select the *minimum* details which are necessary for understanding of the main idea that is expressed in the topic sentence. This exercise should demonstrate to the students that each person needs more or fewer details for understanding of main ideas, depending upon the individual's previous knowledge and experience.

The reader's purpose is of prime importance in comprehending what is read. Is his purpose to get a general impression of the article or is it to seek out useful details that are presently missing? Is it to substantiate a point of view? Are the facts to be used in a report, or is the reader's purpose merely to provide entertainment and enjoyment?

With his purpose for reading clearly in mind, the student should be encouraged to read rapidly to decide whether the material at hand fulfills his purpose. Many students have not learned this phase of the reading act and laboriously read every word of an article only to discover that the material was inapplicable to their purpose. Much has been achieved when the student starts with a definite purpose in mind and skims quickly to decide if he is on the right track.

Once the student locates material that is related to his problem, he should follow a plan somewhat like the following:

1. Reread those portions that have the closest relationship to his problem.
2. Make mental or written notes of the points to be remembered.
3. Summarize the content of the article in his own words.
4. Make a recommendation for action or for use of the ideas. (This step is almost always overlooked as the culmination of the reading activity.)

For students of average or superior ability reading must be more than understanding the stated facts. Good readers should be able to *infer* the author's intent and to predict what will follow. Inference calls for recognition of cause-effect patterns, subtle editorializing or persuasion, exaggeration, or oversimplification. This skill in making inferences is a thinking process and ties directly into past experiences of the reader as he fuses his own ideas with the thoughts of the author. It also has the value of enabling the reader to project the ideas into future plans of action.

Critical reading. The most able students in the secondary school should have frequent opportunity to engage in critical reading. Each new group of high school graduates should add to the general populace a high percentage of readers who are discriminating in their choice of reading material. This can be guaranteed only if they are led through guided discussion to evaluate their readings. They should be able to assess the worth, authenticity, and integrity of each piece of writing. The implication is not that the critical reader will restrict himself to a diet of serious themes; but it does mean that he can discriminate readily among the various levels of reading material. He will recognize the book or magazine that can serve as a mere time filler as he waits for the departure of his plane; he knows which type of book will provide relaxation and enjoyment or which one will extend his knowledge of peoples, places, and events; and he selects with care the book or magazine that will best serve his vocational and personal needs.

Any program of critical reading will include opportunities for students to make comments and criticisms; to compare the treatment of a common theme in two pieces of literature; and to evaluate the depth of plot and the sincerity of characterization in a book, or the artistry of the author. The reader should be led to state honestly the effect of the material on him and to relate his personal reaction even though it differs radically from the interpretation of others.

Précis. Another type of intensive, analytical reading is for the purpose of *making a précis.* A good précis is restated in the words of the reader with no violation of the author's ideas and purposes. Skilled readers and précis writers usually state the main purposes in independent clauses and the details in subordinate clauses. This is an exacting task; it demands intensive concentration, intimate insight into the author's viewpoint, and retention of the sequence and relationship of ideas to the intent of the author. Technical and scientific materials lend themselves to this type of briefing and summarization.

Frederick Davis has identified nine different types of comprehension which should be emphasized in the instructional program of the secondary school. Obviously, they apply to all areas of the curriculum:

1. Selecting appropriate meaning for a word or phrase in context.
2. Following the organization and identifying antecedents and references to it.
3. Selecting the main idea.
4. Determining the answers of questions which are explicitly answered in the passage.
5. Determining the answers of questions answered in the passage and stating those answers in different words.
6. Drawing inferences.
7. Recognizing literary devices.
8. Identifying the tone and mood of a passage.
9. Determining the author's purpose, intent, or viewpoint.[3]

In addition to the discussion which has been directed toward these types of comprehension in this chapter, a more complete development of each type is to be found in the chapters on reading in the content areas.

[3] Frederick B. Davis, "Comprehension in Reading," *Baltimore Bulletin of Education*, XXVIII: 16–24 (January–February, 1951).

Oral Reading

Oral reading is an important phase of any reading program which the secondary student finds many occasions to use in all his subjects. He may want to read a portion of a selection because it has direct application to a discussion; he may seek clarification of a sentence or paragraph that he has encountered; he may wish to call attention to a particularly beautiful passage in literature.

Oral reading has specific characteristics that should be recognized. The listener responds when the reading is rhythmic, varied in speed and emphasis; when full response to the punctuation as a cue to meaning and emotion is evident; and when interpretation brings out mood, emotions, and setting.

Oral reading should not be confused with mere sight reading. Oral reading implies careful preparation and practice before the rendition. The oral reader has the responsibility to his listeners of preparing material so that he can adequately convey the meanings and moods which an author has attempted to portray.

Extensive reading of narrative material is one of the surest ways to gain skill in oral reading. Stress should be placed upon voice-thought correlation. If students read jerkily and fail to speak groups of related words, practice in recognizing thought units may be necessary. One technique which may be used to improve this recognition is to have students underline thought units as they read silently; then the material is more likely to unfold smoothly and meaningfully in oral presentation.

Another means of conveying to students the importance of phrasing and voice quality is through use of the tape recorder. Comparison of a student's oral reading with his natural patterns of speech is almost certain to show whether he needs to improve phrasing, emphasis, and tone quality in his oral reading, which may appear to be highly artificial, with uneven cadence and inappropriate emphasis. Careful preparation for oral reading often helps to eliminate some of these artificial qualities.

If the presentation has been carefully prepared by the student, then he should be encouraged to stand *before* the class for his reading. So often the student becomes discouraged in reading orally because he must direct his reading to the backs of other students' heads; he may then resort to mumbling his lines because he feels oral reading isn't very important. Audience reaction is the greatest motivator for perfection of any communication skill; consequently, students should have many opportunities to test their oral reading skills by the reactions of interested listeners.

The student must differentiate between the two main types of oral reading: the artistic, such as reading poetry, lines in a play, or conversation in a story; and the practical, such as announcements, directions, minutes of a meeting, or a list of items to be checked by his listeners. Each type calls for careful preparation if the reader is to use appropriate voice quality, phrasing, and emphasis. Teachers of all content areas in the secondary school should provide opportunities for their students to read orally.

Locating Information

The skills of locating and selecting information and of subsequently organizing it are commonly referred to as reference skills. These skills represent an entirely different field and one in which the student cannot make his own terms. The secondary school program brings the student face to face with a new type of school program; the likelihood that he is going to need direct help with reference skills is evident.

Skimming is one of the essential skills for the student who must do lengthy assignments or considerable research. While skimming calls for rapid reading, it should not be confused with careless or purposeless reading. Skimming is a precision skill whenever it is used in an effort to locate the exact paragraphs that contain desired information. The reader must be discerning and systematic.

There are various types of skimming which the student must learn to identify, and certain "cues" which are generally useful should be learned:

1. Locating a date or a figure: look for numerals or for numbers which have been written out. When a cue is located, read carefully around it to determine whether this is the desired information.
2. Locating persons' names or geographical locations: look for capitalized words. Read carefully to determine if the correct information has been located.
3. Determining whether a book or periodical contains needed information: skim the table of contents, the index, and subheads within chapters.
4. Seeking information to support or refute a viewpoint: skim the foreword or preface of a book; look for key phrases and sentences in a periodical article; watch carefully for key words that are almost sure to be used.
5. Determining what a book is about: read first and last sentences in paragraphs; stop occasionally to read an entire paragraph intensively. (This skill assumes no previous knowledge of the book or periodical, and no purpose other

than to find out whether a book or article would be interesting either as a source of information or as entertainment.)

Once the student has located several references that he believes to be pertinent to his topic he needs additional skills to aid him in making proper selection. Publication dates are important. If the purpose is to know the latest interpretations and ideas, the most recent publication dates will be sought. On the other hand, if source materials are needed, earlier publications may provide better information. Learning something about the background of the writers also may influence choice of material. The author with firsthand information about a subject may be more reliable than one who writes from collected information; but the former must be notable for his objectivity and freedom from a particular slant or bias.

A student's skimming must be purposeful. He must constantly be guided by a clear purpose whenever he seeks information. Classroom practice in skimming should begin with the simplest forms—the determination of exact dates, place names, and other data—and proceed to the more complex forms, such as trying to discover the viewpoint of a particular author.

Using a book efficiently calls for expert knowledge of nature, structure, and uses of many features of a book: the table of contents; the index; maps, graphs, and illustrations; and special features such as footnotes, the glossary, and the appendix. Some teachers in the secondary school subjects expect skills for using a book efficiently to be taught thoroughly in the elementary grades. Actually, many students will need no further training, but others are simply not prepared to handle the complex textbooks and reference books demanded in the secondary curriculum.

During the first week of a particular course the teacher should take time to examine with the students the textbooks and reference works which will be used in that course. If they seem ill-prepared to use the books, he should set up exercises in the use of the table of contents, index, graphic aids, footnotes, and other aids which are provided by the author of the book. All students should sense the purpose of each part and be able to use it quickly and effectively. Throughout the course the teacher should check to determine how effectively the students are using the helps in the textbook, especially as new features appear. Occasionally he may find it necessary to organize a group of students for further instruction and practice in using them.

Using the library becomes an increasingly important skill as the particular subjects demand greater maturity and increasingly wider reading. Students should be well instructed in the use of the card catalogue, the *Reader's Guide to Periodical Literature,* and similar special-subject guides, the *World Almanac,* fugitive materials, and other library sources.

No high school student can succeed in his study if he is not equipped to use a dictionary, encyclopedias, and atlases expertly. The use of the dictionary requires knowledge of alphabetical sequence, use of the pronunciation guide, and familiarity with such features as phonetic pronunciation, diacritical marks, symbols for parts of speech, and the indicated derivation of words. Typically a dictionary is consulted to determine word meanings, pronunciation, synonyms and antonyms, and, of course, the spelling of the word. Excellent guides for the teaching of the dictionary are available at no charge from the publishers of leading dictionaries.

The encyclopedia, which gives information on an extensive number of topics, constitutes a major reference for the student who is seeking specific information. However, the accounts in encyclopedias must of necessity be comparatively brief and limited in the number of details.

How to use the following features of the encyclopedia should be emphasized:

1. The volume guide—label on back of each book, indicating the scope of major topics treated in each volume
2. Guide words, indicating first and last topics to be found on each page
3. Arrangements—subject headings and subheadings
4. Index volume—indicating which volume contains specific topics
5. Cross indexing—the mention of other articles which contain supplemental information on a topic.

The teacher of English usually assumes responsibility for teaching library skills. With the aid of the librarian he may give students practice in locating and reporting information as they become acquainted with the library:

1. Arrange with the librarian for a guided tour of the library, to point out to students the general classifications of materials and their locations. Follow-up activities could include study and discussion of the Dewey Classification System, entries on the library card, the general location of reference materials, and policies about their use.
2. Assign a narrow topic for research and allow students thirty minutes in the library; when they return, make a cooperative list of all the sources which were used, indicate their location, and suggest other areas of the curriculum which might benefit from use of these particular sources.

3. Assign lessons for reading and discussion in a good library manual. Santa and Hardy's *How to Use the Library* (Pacific Books) is an excellent source for the secondary student.

Speed of Reading

The average secondary student reads too slowly to be efficient in preparing his extended assignments. Many do not read at the speed of which they are capable. On the other hand, an undue emphasis on exercises that induce speed divorced from accompanying understanding could be disastrous in a reading program. It is highly possible that the student can improve his speed of reading in the various content areas, but it is vitally important for him to understand that he must suit his rate to his purpose, the complexity of the treatment, and the familiarity of the material.

The student who makes a conscious effort to read faster will no doubt increase his speed of reading. The easiest material for practice is the narrative type. Once the student has learned to read narrative at an increased rate he may feel encouraged to read other materials faster.

Much of the material a high school student is called upon to read is not straight narration or description. The expository material in science and mathematics calls for intensive, slow reading; social studies material may benefit from a rapid overview, followed by more careful reading. If the purpose is to get a general impression, speed need not be rigidly restricted; on the other hand, if the purpose is to get accurate information for a report, the rate should be slower and the concentration much greater.

There is no single acceptable rate of reading for any

particular content area; hence, an attempt to determine the number of words per minute that a high school student should read is futile. The student who has developed skills of rapid recognition of words and phrases, who has learned to skim a selection in order to familiarize himself with the content, and who has mastered the various skills of comprehension will usually read rapidly. It is important that each student realize the necessity for shifting the rate of reading when greater concentration on details is demanded by the particular content. Perhaps more emphasis upon the number of ideas per page rather than the number of words per page is a more reasonable approach to developing flexibility in rate. A page loaded with main ideas and essential details, obscure concepts, and inferences naturally demands a slower pace.

Many students have never learned to read in terms of thought units. They read word by word and lose the meaning by the time they have finished a complex sentence. A technique which is sometimes successful in teaching students to read by thought units consists of underlining phrases or indicating their limits by diagonal marks:

To develop fluency in reading, one should become aware of the thought units which exist in a sentence.

or

Grasping the natural thought units/ both visually and mentally/ in a sentence/ aids the student/ in speed and comprehension.

Several sets of commercial films have been developed to aid the student in learning to read by thought units: *The Iowa Reading Films* (University of Iowa), *The Harvard*

Reading Films (Harvard University), and a recent series *Phrase Reading* (C-B Educational Films). There is danger that this ability to read by thought units will not transfer from the film to the printed page. The teacher must take care to impress the student with the importance of transferring the skill to actual reading materials. While films such as those mentioned above have high motivational value, they should be used only as a means to an end. They should be made a direct aid in reading book materials, and should not constitute the total reading program.

Teachers should observe students to note those who vocalize excessively, whose concentration is poor, or who fail to follow a consistent method in reading silently. High school students are mature enough to profit from a frank discussion of their faulty habits of reading, which have developed over a long period of time and will not disappear immediately with a mere mention of each particular inadequacy. Constant gentle reminders and favorable comment on each evidence of improvement will in time help students to substitute more efficient patterns. The teacher should also stress with all students the importance of having a purpose for reading and determining, in terms of the purpose and the nature of the reading materials, *how* a selection should be read. After such training, the mature student can make a considered and wise decision as to the speed to be applied to a particular reading assignment.

Summary

A developmental reading program at each level of the secondary school is necessary for continued growth in reading ability. Reading at the secondary level is often complex and technical, requiring both general skills of reading and particular skills demanded in each subject area. A survey of the needs of students should reveal those skills which need further emphasis. Some skills will be found to be under-developed and to require remedial training; others will require frequent practice for maintenance; and still other skills of a more complex kind must be introduced as more advanced types of reading assignments are called for. Every teacher in a high school has definite responsibility for developing reading skills demanded in his particular subject area.

Suggested Readings

DEIGHTON, LEE C. "Developing Vocabulary: Another Look at the Problem," *English Journal*, XLIX (February, 1960), 82–88.

GRAY, WILLIAM S. "Increasing the Basic Reading Competencies of Students," *Reading in the High School and College*. 47th Yearbook, National Society for the Study of Education. Chicago: University of Chicago Press, 1948. Pp. 91–115.

McCULLOUGH, CONSTANCE M. "What Does Research Reveal about Practices in Teaching Reading," *What We Know about High School Reading*. Champaign. Ill.: National Council of Teachers of English, 1957–58. Pp. 19–34.

Reading, Grades 7, 8, 9: A Teacher's Guide to Curriculum Planning. Curriculum Bulletin No. 11, 1957–58 Series. New York: Board of Education of the City of New York, 1959.

ROBERTS, CLYDE. *Word Attack: A Way to Better Reading*. New York: Harcourt, Brace and Co., 1956.

WITTY, PAUL. "An Articulated Program for Teaching Reading Skills from Kindergarten to College," *Bulletin of the National Association of Secondary-School Principals*, XXXIX (September, 1955), 7–14.

The Suggestion Box

As a means of determining the phonetic and structural analysis difficulties which students experience, you, as a teacher, can prepare a list of words which contains examples of phonetic and structural elements. As students take turns in pronouncing these words, mark the errors on a master sheet. Give a list of words to be spelled (written) and analyze errors for phonetic and structural misunderstandings. On the basis of the errors discovered, prepare exercises and class discussions to correct the errors.

Encourage students to build individual vocabulary lists for each content area. If appropriate, allow time once a week for discussion of new words which students have encountered in their reading or in listening to radio, television and conversation.

Select several books on vocabulary and general language development; encourage students to read these and to involve other students in class exercises based on their reading (see Appendix D).

Examine, with students, newspaper and periodical articles to locate emotionally flavored and qualifying words. Discuss these, both in terms of the context and other uses of the words.

Occasionally set a purpose for reading a particular passage in a textbook: reading for details, reading for a main idea, discovering new words, skimming for a generalization, etc. Encourage students to discuss the difficulties they encountered.

VII

How to Study in Every Subject

THE STUDENT WHO ENTERS THE JUNIOR OR SENIOR high school is faced with new problems. Wider reading is required in specific content areas; more intensive study is demanded as each subject increases in complexity; not so much individual attention is possible in the classroom, since many teachers in the content subjects meet at least five different groups of students each day. To be successful in his work the student must necessarily develop independence in his study habits.

Many young people and adults who are excellent readers of literary materials still fail in school, because they have not learned to concentrate and *think* while reading informational materials or because they lack effective study habits. Good study habits depend not only upon a knowledge of sound procedures in attacking factual materials but also upon the ability to decide just what skills or habits are applicable to the situation or the particular assignment. Setting a purpose for reading, skimming, reading intensively, and reacting to what is read are, as we have seen, classified as *reading* skills; certainly the whole body of reading skills might further be classified as a part of study skills. However, the term *study skills* refers further to the application of reading skills to specific study tasks, organizing and scheduling one's time for study, taking good notes, and preparing for and taking examinations.

While we recognize that a general body of study skills and habits is basic to success in all content areas, each content area also requires specific study skills. The teacher of a particular subject is, practically, the one to give the methods best for that subject. The teacher of English generally assumes the responsibility for teaching reference skills, note taking, précis writing, and selective reading. But the science teacher also should feel a responsibility for impressing his students with the importance of specific skills needed for the science area. The English teacher is generally not trained to teach the student the particular skills for studying science and mathematics; yet traditionally he has been the only teacher in the secondary school who has been concerned about these skills which are so vital to the students' efficiency; or, if teachers of other subjects have felt any concern, they have considered it the English teacher's responsibility to give the training. The point is that he is often not equipped to do so, and even if he were, the teacher of science or social studies should assume a share of the responsibility.

Surveying the assignment. Each day in the classroom failures occur because assignments are misunderstood, ignored, or forgotten; because the student, confronted by a long assignment, feels that it is futile to attempt the task; or because there is no clear-cut starting point for studying the assignment. Teachers can aid the student in clarifying the assignment by:

1. Giving a brief introduction to the assignment and relating it, if possible, to previous learning or experiences of the students.
2. Pointing out the new or technical vocabulary.
3. Stating *exactly* what is required of the student as he carries out the assignment.
4. Giving references through which the students may gain needed background, broader understanding, or greater depth.

The student may improve his ability to handle daily assignments by:

1. Keeping a calendar of assignments—a small notebook in which he records the assignment for each subject and jots down suggestions given by the teacher, such as specific references and vocabulary.
2. Listening carefully to learn just what is expected of him in this assignment and writing down the directions given by the teacher.
3. Selecting an exact time and place for studying the assignment. (Few students realize the importance of becoming psychologically oriented to studying. If they learn to establish a time and place for studying each subject each day they soon discover that they are actually ready to begin work when they reach their familiar place of study.)
4. Surveying the chapter or pages to be read. (Thomas Staton uses the intriguing PQRST symbols to indicate a method of surveying a chapter: preview, question, read, state, and test.[1]) The process, fundamentally, is this:
   a. Preview the assignment. Read the title carefully; think about what it covers or to what it refers. What previous

[1] Thomas Staton, *How to Study* (Nashville, Tenn.: McQuiddy Publishing Co., 1955).

knowledge do you have of this topic? How can it be related to what you've just covered? Now read *intensively*
the introductory paragraph and the summary paragraph,
if there is one. Read each subtitle.

b. Question. As you read the titles, subtitles, and summary
   paragraphs, ask yourself questions which you think will
   be answered by the selection. Read the first and last
   sentences of paragraphs and pose questions which arise
   as you read.

c. Read. Look carefully for answers to your questions. Read
   intensively those parts with which you have not
   had previous experience or knowledge. Read rapidly
   those parts which merely expand ideas which you
   already understand. Note any novel attitudes or viewpoints.

d. State. Turn quickly through the chapter or selection, and
   work at stating precisely the answers to your questions.
   Attempt to state the main ideas and at least two or three
   subordinate points under each. Doing this gives you a
   mental framework of the author's statements and indicates where you have not yet attained adequate understanding.

e. Test. Go back and read *intensively* those areas which are
   not yet clear to you. Now test yourself again on the
   "state" step.

If the student is stimulated by this technique he will find
it an excellent concentration device. He may become sufficiently involved in questions and answers that good reading
results—and in a minimum of time, since rereading is seldom
necessary.

Now the student should feel encouraged to turn to additional references for further clarification or expansion of the
ideas encountered, plus comparisons and contrasts which can
be used to shed light on the assignment.

Reading selectively. Many conscientious students, when confronted with a reading task, become anxious and read more than is actually required. The result is a waste of time and in many cases a confusion of ideas. It is preferable that he do selective reading that is purposeful. If he knows definitely what he is seeking he can read intensively with true economy of time and effort.

In the reading of reference materials selective reading is of utmost value. The reader must keep clearly in mind the information sought and systematically discard any material that is irrelevant or unimportant. The tendency in unskilled research reading is to immerse oneself in extraneous materials —intriguing and challenging as they may be—and to lose sight of the goal that is the purpose of the reading.

An interesting teaching technique for developing skill in reading selectively is as follows: Select a narrow topic and allow ten minutes for the research; then ask students to report the pertinent information they have gleaned. Record all this on the chalkboard as it is offered. Now ask the students to volunteer other information, on unrelated topics, which they gained through their research. Write this down too. Often several students will find that they have collected more unrelated information than pertinent facts. An analysis of this situation will identify the distractors which are encountered as a student attempts to do selective reading.

To emphasize potency of distractors, have the students examine the placement of advertisements in a periodical. Advertisers pay premium prices for strategic positions of their advertisements in periodicals and journals, because they realize the power of the distractor on the reader.

When students come to realize that selective reading requires a clear-cut purpose and the utmost concentration they have taken their first steps toward the development of this skill.

Note taking. There is no greater waste of time and energy by students than that of note taking as it is generally practiced. So many students begin the semester with a fresh notebook, a desire to take good notes, and the determination to use those notes. What happens to this positive beginning which we observe in so many of our classes? The students lack the requisite skills in note taking. Notes are taken sketchily and never reorganized; the desire to keep abreast of the minimum requirements of the course fades quickly in the face of this disorganization; and because most notes are found unusable, the notebook is carelessly laid aside.

No skill requires more careful instruction and supervision than that of note taking; yet it is difficult for a teacher to determine exact standards. An able student will develop his own efficient system. However, each subject-matter teacher should assume that many students in the class are as yet incapable of taking good notes, and instruction should be given for his particular subject. He should lead preliminary discussion of the importance and methods of note taking, in which students are encouraged to voice their opinions and share their experiences on the subject. Guidelines should be set up; the instructor should give a well-organized but short lecture so that the students can practice taking notes. Then they are asked to compare their notes and to work as a group in reorganizing the notes. Another technique, a variation on the above, is to give a lecture with many facts irrelevant to the announced subject. After the notes have been compared and reorganized, each student is to check his notes to find if he included any irrelevant material.

Taking good notes serves to keep the student alert and to increase his participation. His notes provide a means of reviewing information; they aid in establishing meaningful relationships between ideas gathered from many sources; they provide a means of checking on the accuracy of the speaker or writer when further research is done; and they encourage the organization and retention of ideas. Here are a few points for aiding students in improving their note-taking skills:

1. Be ready to take notes when you enter class. Have pen or pencil and notebook ready.
2. Organize your notebook so that each subject has its own special section. Use a loose-leaf notebook so that you can insert assignment sheets, syllabi, and other helpful materials as they come to hand.
3. Listen more and write less. Select leading ideas. Do not attempt to write verbatim the words of the lecturer. The notes will be more meaningful if they are in your own words.
4. If a point is missed, ask the lecturer to repeat or check with another student at the end of the period.
5. As soon as possible after the class, look over the notes; reorganize and rewrite them. Underline important points for future reference.
6. Review your notes periodically.[2]

Preparing for and taking examinations. The secondary school usually places heavy emphasis upon examinations, but

---

[2] For a more thorough discussion of these skills, see Henry A. Bamman and Lawrence M. Brammer, *How to Study Successfully* (Palo Alto, Calif.: Pacific Books, 1959).

many students have never before been required to take examinations of the type given in most subject areas. They need guidance in how to prepare for and take tests; they need to understand the fundamental purposes and values of examinations.

The examination should serve several purposes:

1. A reviewing device to aid in learning and to provide an incentive for further study.
2. A checking device to determine if the student has done the required work.
3. A measuring device to determine how well the student has mastered the subject area.
4. A means of measuring the effectiveness of instruction.
5. A means of assigning grades to the individual students.

It is not our purpose to provide criteria by which the teacher can write good examinations. It is sufficient to state that many classroom examinations are carefully prepared and fulfill the purposes for which they were written, but many others fall woefully short of providing anything except busy work.

There certainly should be a balance between objective and essay-type examinations, since each type of test may measure a different skill. The recognition, or objective, type of test is measuring recall of specific details and data or the recognition of principles or ideas. The essay test should measure the understanding of key ideas and their relationships, the application of principles or ideas, and the student's ability to express himself. Once the student knows the type of examination to be given (and the teacher should inform the student that a certain type is to be given) he governs his study accordingly.

Certain procedures have been followed successfully by students in taking examinations:

1. Objective type: true-false, multiple-choice, matching:
   a. Glance over the exam to determine the number of items and determine the requirements in terms of time allotted.
   b. Read the directions carefully; note the type of marking system which is required.
   c. Start with item one and mark only those items which you are confident you know. Skip difficult items and come back to them later; a subsequent item may give you a helpful hint for the perplexing one.
   d. Do not change an answer unless you have further information.
   e. Beware of such statements as "always," "never," and "only." These are often the qualifiers which determine the correctness or incorrectness of the statement.
2. Essay type:
   a. Read through all questions carefully. If you may choose which questions to answer, make that choice immediately. Determine the amount of time that each will require.
   b. Outline an answer briefly before you write. It is a good idea to open an essay answer with a summary statement; then state supporting details and summarize in different words.
   c. Do not feel that essay questions must be written in the order in which they are given. If you do not know the answer to one question, go on to another. This answer may give you a lead to the one which has puzzled you.
   d. Avoid verbosity. Write concisely and clearly. Be neat in your writing. (While good handwriting is not necessarily a criterion of a good answer, legibility does influence the person who grades the paper.[3])

[3] *Ibid.*

It is a good idea for students to record on their assignment sheets the dates of announced examinations. You should encourage your students to space review over a period of several days or periods before the test is scheduled, rather than to attempt to "cram" the night before the examination.

Scheduling. Spacing short study periods throughout the week or month is more conducive to good learning and retention than attempting to cram everything into one long period. However, the length of the study period, and its frequency, will naturally depend upon the subject.

When a student takes an objective look at the time he wastes each day, simply because he is lost in the milieu of unplanned activities, he should become aware of the necessity for establishing some type of schedule. The teacher may need to guide him to this realization. He will learn, once he has followed a schedule, that he will accomplish more in less time and that he will have some carefree hours left over. To impress the student with the necessity for scheduling his class and study periods, the teacher may suggest that he keep an accurate account of everything he does for a forty-eight-hour period. During this time he should avoid changing his usual routine. As a consequence, many students will immediately see that they waste countless hours each day and that their inefficiency yields only personal dissatisfaction. They are then in a mood to welcome suggestions on scheduling their study time and setting up a routine that will yield good results.

No one can expect every student to follow exactly the same schedule, since a good schedule should be tailored to the unique needs of the individual. But these general suggestions are usually helpful to all students:

1. Set up your schedule to include classes, study hours, and all recreation activities.
2. Set up your schedule for at least two weeks ahead.
3. Limit study on a particular subject to periods of about two hours. Beyond that, there are diminishing returns. If you need more than two hours, turn to another subject for a time and then return to the first one.
4. Plan for periodic review of all subjects. You will find that good review can eliminate those last-minute "jitters" which so many students feel just before a recitation or a test.
5. Keep some periods open for those activities which cannot be anticipated: rallies, committee meetings, and similar activities.
6. Regard your schedule as a flexible instrument. You may need to shift some parts of the schedule as emergencies arise.
7. If the schedule which you have made does not work, try others until you have found one which yields the greatest efficiency and satisfaction for you as a student.[4]

Summary

While we are primarily concerned with the improvement of the reading skills of our students, it must be recognized that skills of application are necessary if the student is to be successful. Many students who are excellent readers fail in subjects in our schools because they have poor study habits; conversely, many relatively poor readers achieve better results in the classroom because they have learned good study habits which may compensate, in part, for their lack of reading ability.

Each content area requires both general and specific study skills, and a teacher is responsible for guiding students in

[4] *Ibid.*

the development of skills which will increase their efficiency in that subject. The skills of reading the specific textbook, doing selective reading, taking good notes, preparing for and taking examinations, and scheduling adequate and effective study periods are all integral parts of any content area in the secondary school. The teacher of the individual subject area might well spend several days at the beginning of each academic period in acquainting the students with the particular skills that are necessary for successful achievement in the subject area and in giving practice in those skills. The possibilities for improved learning are great.

Suggested Readings

ARMSTRONG, W. H. *Study Is Hard Work.* New York: Harper and Brothers, 1956.

BAMMAN, HENRY A., and BRAMMER, LAWRENCE M. *How to Study Successfully.* Palo Alto, Calif.: Pacific Books, 1959.

HARDY, LOIS LYNN. *How to Study in High School.* Palo Alto, Calif.: Pacific Books, 1954.

MORGAN, CLIFFORD T., and DEESE, JAMES. *How to Study.* New York: McGraw-Hill Book Co., 1957.

STATON, THOMAS. *How to Study.* Nashville, Tenn.: McQuiddy Publishing Co., 1955.

The Suggestion Box

Before handing examinations back to students, make a list of the most common errors that have been made in terms of completeness, irrelevancies, lack of organization, lack of specific details, etc. Read to the class outstanding examples from good papers and discuss, in a positive manner, the skills required for writing good exams.

Give an occasional "open-book" examination to determine (1) ability to read a question and sense its intent and (2) ability to locate and select relevant answers.

Occasionally, following a lecture-discussion period, ask several students to review their notes for the benefit of the other class members. Compare and contrast the note-taking abilities of members of the class and give suggestions for the improvement of skills in this critical area.

Periodically, ask students to list problems they have had in studying for a particular assignment. Include such factors as accessibility of reference materials, note taking, scheduling of time for studying, clarity of purpose, use of cross references, clarity of teacher's assignment.

VIII

The Social Studies

OF THE SO-CALLED ACADEMIC SUBJECTS THE SOCIAL studies probably make the greatest demand on reading time. It is safe to say that this academic field requires from one fourth to one third of all the time spent in reading in the junior and senior high schools, especially since the social studies are offered in all grades from seven to twelve.

The Committee on Social Studies of the Commission on the Reorganization of Secondary Education of the National Education Association in 1916 defined the term *social studies:* "The social studies are understood to be those whose subject matter relates directly to the organization and development of human society, and to man as a member of social groups." [1] In the secondary curriculum this branch of instruction includes: history, geography, civics, economics, sociology, and current events—all with the common goal of developing

---

[1] United States Bureau of Education, *The Social Studies in Secondary Education,* Bulletin, 1916, No. 28 (Washington, D.C.: Government Printing Office, 1928), p. 1.

active participation in the affairs of a democracy by an enlightened citizenry.

Edgar Bruce Wesley in *Teaching the Social Studies* states:

Every teacher of the social studies recognizes the importance of an intensive and extensive reading program. In no subject except possibly English is the reading program more fundamental. The area of desirable experience in the social studies is practically unlimited, and the area of actual experience is necessarily quite limited. Reading offers practically the only means by which the students can, at least vicariously acquire all the rich and illuminating experiences which the human race has had.[2]

Reading in the social studies is more difficult than the reading of narrative material to which the student has typically become accustomed in his daily "reading" assignments at the elementary school level. The content of the typical social studies textbook is condensed; vocabulary is not controlled and is more difficult than in literature; the student is required to read and organize a mass of seemingly unrelated facts and to organize them in proper relationships; the ideas are complex and require wide reading for clarification; much supplementary material is necessary for full appreciation of persons and events; previous knowledge must be recalled to illuminate ideas and develop depth of concepts.

Ernest Horn in his *Methods of Instruction in the Social Studies* indicates the difficulties the student encounters in reading a typical social studies textbook:

Many of the ideas presented in typical textbooks in geography, history, or other social studies are so intrinsically complicated that they would be difficult to understand even if described in liberal detail, in untechnical language, and in a lucid, attractive

[2] Edgar Bruce Wesley, *Teaching the Social Studies* (Boston: D. C. Heath and Co., 1942), p. 306.

style. Actually however they are presented in the form of condensed and abstract statements that are readily understood only by those who have already formed the generalization for which the statements stand.[3]

If social studies material presents such problems as indicated, what can the social studies department of a secondary school do to modify the situation? In the book *Aspects of Readability in the Social Studies,* the author has proposed some ways of meeting the problem:

1. Evaluate the readability of each textbook.
2. Demonstrate to students how to read the textbook effectively.
3. Help the students to use all of the context clues that the book contains.
4. Give serious consideration to the use of multi-texts to meet the varying reading abilities.[4]

Although we refer to the social studies as a "block" of learning materials, the simple fact is that we are still teaching history, geography, economics, sociology, civics, and other related areas; and each of these areas requires a specific skill or group of skills of efficient reading. Each of the subjects in the social studies is written in a different way, simply because the authors' experience has dictated that they *should* be written in a fashion peculiarly appropriate to each particular subject. Geography, for instance, is not presented in a narrative form. It includes naming a nation and locating it in reference to other nations; it enumerates racial and ethnic groups within certain boundaries, the products of the region,

[3] Ernest Horn, *Methods of Instruction in the Social Studies* (New York: Scribner, 1937), pp. 157–58.

[4] Eleanor M. Peterson, *Aspects of Readability in the Social Studies* (New York: Bureau of Publications, Teachers College, Columbia University, 1954), pp. 34–35.

a description of the physical features, discussion of the natural and manufactured products, their distribution, and effect on the economic life of the people; it relates location, climate, cultural development, and living standards as factors in the adaptation of people to their environment. Such breadth of information is conveyed through place names, technical terms, and geographical concepts in such abundance that the student may well be confused as to which is important and which is unimportant. If pronouncing and remembering the name of a particular seaport or mountain range is relevant to understanding of the unit being studied, then it is important. But in the highly condensed type of writing done in geography place names are often introduced and never mentioned again.

It should be clear that students reading in the social studies should be able to relate what they read to their own background of experiences and previous learnings. This means, of course, that textbooks should be selected to bridge the gap between the background experiences of students and the rather technical and difficult concepts which the students are expected to comprehend and master. In view of the heterogeneity of students in the typical social studies class (heterogeneous in terms of interests, skills, and experiences), no single textbook can meet the needs of those students. Teachers have a responsibility for guiding students into wide reading in supplementary materials, in making available several texts of varying difficulty, and in developing accurate and critical listening skills so that class discussion and reporting may strengthen reading skills.

The textbook is a very compact and somewhat complicated product, the most expeditious use of which requires considerable understanding and skill. Some of its most helpful features require explanation and drill if they are to yield maximum values. Since so much time and attention are devoted to textbooks, the teacher should see that pupils learn how to utilize them most advantageously.[5]

For example, in most modern textbooks the content is divided into units, with several chapters to a unit. If the author's organization includes a preview of the unit with advance notice of persons and events that will be important to that section, time is well spent if the teacher introduces the textbook by calling attention to such previews and their helpfulness in study. In the same way headings, illustrations, cartoons, charts, maps, and tables should be shown to be means which the author has used to clarify his discourse. At the end of chapters or units the authors of textbooks may call attention to important terms to be remembered; make a brief summary of the material; include questions for review or discussion; suggest activities for groups or individuals; and list books, magazines, and source material that will add to the understanding and appreciation of a particular phase of development. The class and the teacher should discuss each of these study helps and decide on how to use each feature effectively in study. Cooperative effort of this kind will repay many times the hours it has taken. If the class follows through the use of these study aids for one unit, when the next section is studied the student will understand how each part can contribute to his grasp of the particular problem.

It is evident that teaching in the social studies demands more than the dissemination of facts and figures. A back-

[5] Wesley, *op. cit.*

ground of knowledge, based on facts and experiences, is obviously necessary for good reading in the social studies; but careful attention to the basic skills of reading for good comprehension of history, geography, and other areas should be an integral part of the teaching. The identity of these skills and suggestions for their development were presented, in part, in Chapter VI. Specific to the social studies, however, are supplementary understandings and skills that require direct teaching in the social studies class.

Vocabulary. The vocabulary of the social studies is, as we have mentioned, complex, and careful guidance in the development of vocabulary skill is basic to good teaching of any of the subject areas included in the social studies.

1. *Technical terms.* Many terms are specific to the area studied and appear practically nowhere else in the student's reading. For example, a course in English history may introduce such terms as *feudalism, vassal, primogeniture, guild,* and *crusade.* The student's understanding of technical terms depends upon his ability to recognize and pronounce words, to examine the context for clues to the meaning of the words, and to use the dictionary.

2. *Multisyllabic words.* Many long words cause trouble because the student has not become accustomed to looking for familiar elements or because he may not have developed skill in pronunciation. Root elements and derived forms abound in our language; but the pronunciation and understanding of the derived form may prove to be relatively simple if the student learns to seek root forms, as in *total*itarian, *account*ability, tele*communicat*ion, phil*anthrop*ic *endow*ments. Each of these words may present a formidable appearance to the student; yet each is simple in pronunci-

ation and not difficult in terms of its meaning *if* careful scrutiny is given to each.

3. *Abstract words. Liberty, justice, equality, democracy,* and *despotism* are words whose meaning develops slowly as the student matures and sees application of each to everyday experiences or reads of examples of each in past history. The word in and of itself is virtually meaningless until it is applied to experience or previous knowledge, which makes it meaningful to the individual. The teacher must be aware that the meanings of many of our abstract words develop on a continuum and that exact definitions are not nearly so desirable as the ability and tendency to make varied applications to situations and experiences.

4. *General terms.* Social studies, like many other subject areas, make use of words that are in the general vocabulary but have a specific and different connotation in this area. Attaching a familiar but inappropriate meaning to such terms may spell the difference between confusion and understanding. For example, mentioning grain elevators in the Great Lakes region can easily be a meaningless concept to students who associate the term *elevator* with the usual denotation of a passenger carrier. Any important word that has multiple meanings should be checked with a class to make certain that the idea associated with the term is clear.

5. *Mathematical terms.* The content of any of the branches of the social studies will make rather extensive use of mathematical vocabulary and expressions. Time designations, area, population statistics, graphs, and charts need to be discussed and clarification made when necessary.

6. *Concepts.* The concept is more than a word or group of words. It is a mental image, an abstraction, which results as

the individual generalizes from particulars. The depth of a concept for an individual depends not only upon his direct experience but also upon his intelligence and his maturity. The child develops concepts as his direct and vicarious experiences broaden, and there is no limit to the concept as the child matures and is capable of modifying or changing his ideas of a particular thing. For example, a child's concept of *tolerance* may at first be very narrow, since even the simplest areas of human relations demand some tolerance of people and things. As he matures he learns that this word is used often to refer to religions of other peoples, to differences in race and color, to ideas and value systems. The complexity of the concept may increase, but broadened experience and knowledge may even so serve to simplify the individual's ideas. The teacher can never assume that the child understands everything presented in apparently simple language which is immediately understandable to the adult. This language actually may represent concepts that are meaningless to the inexperienced young student, and the teacher will need to give concrete examples and use visual aids, later to provide wide reading that will lend rich meaning to such concepts. One note of warning should be injected here, however. Excessive breadth of knowledge may prove to be confusing; what is desired is the clarification of knowledge; consequently, the teacher cannot assume that multiple details and increased vocabulary are actually aiding young people in the process of conceptualizing. The teacher must use good judgment in selecting only those details which will actually aid the student in developing clear concepts in the social studies.

Reading and deriving meaning from long and complex

sentences. Much of the writing for the social studies is compressed and terse; sentences tend to be lengthy and complex in structure. Words and ideas may be introduced, not to be mentioned again; the author may unwisely assume that the students have had previous experiences and learnings that enable them to understand a selection. Here is an example of a fairly difficult sentence:

> The web of social groups that constitutes society is no more of a crazy quilt than the culture followed by the groups; obviously, various groups have specialized functions and are related to other groups because of these functions.[6]

Several words in this sentence may prove to be difficult for the student: *web, society, crazy quilt, culture, specialized functions.* Each word is understood as it refers to previous knowledge or experience. *Web* and *crazy quilt* are used figuratively; *society, culture,* and *specialized functions* require considerable definition and clarification through examples to convey clear meaning in this particular sentence. The teacher of the social studies should be aware of this difficulty in the reading that the average student is required to do or may do on his own. Time should be devoted to reading portions of social studies material to find examples of figurative and symbolic language. One of the major difficulties presented by figurative language is that the comparison may be one completely unrelated to the modern world and hence meaningless to today's youth.

Reading important ideas and developing skill for retention of relevant events and developments. Much of the reading of social studies materials is done in research-type

[6] Harold Rugg and William Withers, *Social Foundations of Education* New York: Prentice-Hall, 1955), p. 541.

sources; in fact, the student often seeks information in a half dozen sources before he finds material that is relevant to his purpose for reading. The identification of the main idea is, of course, a first consideration; important details are later considered in order to explain or further develop the main idea. The student must perceive the headings, marginal topics, and topic sentences as guides that lead to the major point the author is making. Social studies teachers need to ascertain through class exercise whether students are organizing their thinking in this way as they read.

He [the teacher] anticipates the central thought of sections and paragraphs from headings or topic sentences, asks himself questions, pauses to identify proper name, disputes the author's view and then concedes the point or resolves to look it up later; he rewords phrases to improve them or make them his own, interprets details in terms of his own experience or previous reading, and questions the use of a complex term or guesses at its meaning and derives it from context. He relates the material he is reading to the larger area under consideration and to contemporary events. Upon reading the name of an unfamiliar place he locates it, either on a wall map or by reference to known places. At the end of the reading he summarizes the content, fits it into the unit, and comments on its significance to modern living. He may turn to the end of the chapter and identify such terms and answer such questions from the text as relate to the passage studied.[7]

When the teacher has gone through one or two paragraphs in this way it is advisable to discuss the various points that were demonstrated. Did the students recognize that the main idea was determined? Did they notice the time taken

[7] *How to Use a Textbook*, No. 2 of How to Do It Series of the National Council for the Social Studies (Washington, D.C., 1950), p. 5.

to focus on the name of an important person or place? Did they observe the teacher's behavior when a difficult idea was met in the reading? Did they recognize the importance of locating an unfamiliar place immediately so that its relationship to the rest of the material was established immediately? Did they notice that the reading was not completed until the instructor had summarized what he had read, had connected it with the rest of the content, and had attempted to establish a connection between what he had read and present-day activities? Did they grasp the value of referring to the end-of-chapter features as another study skill to aid in retention of the material read?

One of the reasons for the present trend toward integrated social studies areas is that of relevancy of ideas in terms of time, place, or situation. The unit plan of instruction is based on the assumption that ideas are related and that learning is enhanced by emphasizing these relationships. The stereotyped daily-assignment routine of the classroom often develops nothing more than "bit pickers" and "fact locators" of students who read history or geography or civics merely to digest and regurgitate unrelated pieces of information to satisfy the requirements of a particular course. The teacher of the social studies has a responsibility, on the basis of adult knowledge and experience, of establishing relationships among the many ideas that are encountered in a single social studies lesson. Consider, for example, a brief essay on Robert Fulton. The inventor at one time in his life met Benjamin Franklin, a philanthropist, author, and statesman, who encouraged Fulton to go to England to study art under Benjamin West, a leading portrait painter of that era. While in England, Fulton experimented with the torpedo and steamboat and became acquainted with Napoleon (who desired a destructive instrument to be used against the British) and Robert Livingston (who furnished the funds for Fulton's experiments). At this same time in history Beethoven was composing some of the world's greatest music and dedicated one of his symphonies to Napoleon. Scientists, such as Spallanzani, were disputing authority by upsetting the theory of spontaneity of life; defiance of authority was dangerous at a time when Napoleon had declared himself to be omnipotent. Yet the works of Fulton and Napoleon and Spallanzani and dozens of men like them lighted a flame of independence and inquiry that colored the developments of the early nineteenth century. This is but one example of inextricable relationships that exist in the mass of the social studies.

Teachers are aware that students do not learn to relate what they read to experience nor do they learn to retain and organize learnings merely by reading an assignment. Direct teaching involving experiences of wide reading, discussion, and research is vital to the development of skills, organization, and retention of ideas.

Locating and evaluating materials. Because no single textbook is sufficient for the development of a social studies unit, a critical skill demanded of the student is the location and evaluation of relevant materials that expand the knowledge about a topic, give insight into problems, and suggest possible solutions to problems. The teacher of the social studies will be a key person in developing lifelong habits of finding and using supplementary materials. There are four important areas in which the social studies teacher will guide student learning of basic research skills:

1. *Gathering, organizing, and interpreting data* from books, charts, magazines, newspapers, films, television, radio, lectures, fugitive material, and other sources. Skills of reading, analyzing, reacting, reflecting, and criticizing are necessary.

2. *Defining and analyzing* the problems often cannot be satisfactorily accomplished until some research has been done. The student should know whether he actually *has* a problem to pursue, the extent to which he must pursue knowledge in order to satisfy the purposes for which he is working, and the relevancy of other fields of knowledge. The teacher has the responsibility of aiding students in defining problems precisely and clearly and of helping them in locating materials that will suggest possible solutions to the problems.

3. *Utilizing library facilities* depends upon competence in using the library. Chapter VI has introduced the techniques that the teacher might use in aiding students to develop skills in the use of the library. Equally as important is competency in recognizing the reliability and accuracy of library sources. High school students, and even adults, tend to accept that which is in print. The library is seen as a source for locating indisputably authoritative statements in print, whereas much of the material available there is neither accurate nor worthwhile. The social studies teacher should aid students in developing criteria by which source materials may be judged.

4. *Reading maps, tables, graphs, charts,* and *formulas* is not a simple skill despite the fact that many students give evidence of proficiency in location skills. Merely locating information is insufficient, obviously, since determining or

establishing the relationship of the information to the problem at hand is the real task.

Efficient reading of maps requires a knowledge of the different types of maps: thermal, topographical, cultural, global, and magnetic. Each may employ a different scale and different symbols (letters, numbers, colors). The student must learn the meaning of *longitude, latitude,* directions, and those words that designate parts of the globe: *hemisphere, continent, oceans, poles, region,* and others. Essential to the student is the *reason* for having maps in the social studies books; this reason is established only through relationships of the information contained in the text and the information given by the map itself.

Charts, tables, and graphs are often explained in the elementary social studies and arithmetic programs, but the information of the secondary social studies conveyed by such instruments is more detailed, complex, and profuse than in the elementary books. From the beginning of the year's work the teacher should direct some questions that will require the students to abstract information from such sources. It might be well to use the open-book type of class discussion to focus attention on the value of tables, charts, and graphs. In open-book examinations the teacher should also pose a question or two that will require the students to use such illustrative materials in order to answer a question fully.

Comprehending a sequence of events, simultaneous events, and cause-effect relationships. Relationships among events in history are often most easily established through a chronological table or time line. It is possible that a student may have accurate and detailed knowledge of many events in history and never relate those events in terms of their sequence or of their occurrence at the same time in different parts of the world. The example given in this chapter with reference to Robert Fulton illustrates time and event relationships that aid students in understanding the *why* and *how* of social studies. The *who, what,* and *where* factors of any event or historical movement are not so difficult to locate and associate if the *how* and *why* are added.

Cause-effect relationships cannot be fully established unless all these factors have been considered. The *industrial revolution,* for example, should be connected with rise of factories, urban development, unemployment, immigration, development of trade unions, specialization in certain geographic areas, and other related ideas as a basis for the student's understanding the contemporary change due to *automation.*

Discriminating between fact and opinion. Students tend to regard the written word as infallible and to accept it without question. One of the most difficult skills for the student of social studies to develop is the ability to think for oneself and on the basis of this to accept or reject written ideas or theories. Critical reading ability can be developed through experiences that give students practice in perceiving relationships.

1. Comparing sources of information and determining whether the source is original or secondary may be helpful. The student may attempt to find contradictory accounts by different authors, or different points of view expressed by rival editors of newspapers. Along with reports in newspapers it is useful to compare material from government publications. Many of the publications of the federal government are reliable, quite objective in handling data, and a

source of factual information as contrasted with biased opinion. The secondary social studies student should certainly be informed about the availability of federal, state, county, and municipal publications and to see in them an extraordinary resource for obtaining information.

In helping students to compare sources of information the teacher should examine with students the reasons behind many publications, the reputation of the author, the audience to which the publication is directed, the time in which it was written, whether it is the original copyright or a revised edition, and the real purpose for which it was intended.

2. Considering information in terms of previous knowledge or beliefs may aid the students in developing objectivity. The good reader is prepared to change his point of view, often discard a preconceived notion, or find support for what he believes. He must regard new information in terms of its being possible or probable and search further to determine whether or not the information is accurate.

3. Finding and recognizing propaganda devices is important to every citizen, since propaganda is used both negatively and positively. Advertising abounds in propaganda devices, but so do partisan writings, editorials, and all other types of materials for popular consumption. The teacher should give practice to the students in recognizing such devices as name calling, glittering generalities, identification, band-wagon techniques, and others. The main purpose of the teaching of the social studies is to aid students in becoming responsible citizens; certainly the analysis of propaganda is a skill that the citizen needs throughout his lifetime.

Some work on getting an elementary understanding of propaganda should be part of the reading program in the secondary school. One of the easiest ways to lay the foundations for analysis of what is read is the comparison of reporting of the same incident by various newspapers and magazines. What was the headline in the various accounts? What parts of the incident or event received major emphasis in each article? Were some facts omitted in some of the articles? Where was the article placed in the paper or magazine? Did the paper include editorial as well as reporting about the incident? A few questions such as these will help students to realize the pressures that the citizen faces each day.

4. Another simple device is the development of a set of statements to which students are asked to respond in terms of fact and opinion. For example:

1. The purchase of Alaska was the most beneficial of any land acquisitions by the United States; contrasted with
2. Alaska entered the Union as the forty-ninth state

will establish a basis for students' becoming critical of what they read.

Much confusion exists regarding the relative worth of facts and opinions. Facts are established through historical precedence, experimental evidence, and direct observation; but the mere memorization of facts may be worthless to the student, since a fact is valuable only as it has reference to a goal or a problem. There is a tendency among students to regard opinions as worthless, when as a matter of fact our great court decisions are nothing more than opinions, *based on facts or a precedent of worthwhile opinions.* The secondary school student needs to be encouraged to examine facts and opinions and to determine their relative values to his own development as a thinking, acting citizen. Students should recognize that honest differences of opinion are essential in the workings of a democracy.

Drawing conclusions and making sound inferences and generalizations. After the student has learned to select main ideas and relevant details from his reading, he often must be taught to draw conclusions about what he has read. If he reads with an awareness of the relationship of ideas, seeks to determine the accuracy of statements and their bearing on his problem, and then relates that information to his previous knowledge or experience, he may be capable of drawing conclusions. Reading between the lines, or inferring what the author has failed to state directly, is essentially an adult skill and the student develops this skill but gradually. On the other hand, an author will often imply ideas that are necessary for the student's drawing a reasonable conclusion. Obviously, then, the teacher should, through simple exercises, aid the student in learning to infer meanings. No unit in the social studies should be culminated until students and teachers have had an opportunity to state and record conclusions from the information and activities that were pursued in that unit.

Speed. The social studies teacher needs to discuss the matter of speed of reading with the students. Since much of the material in the secondary social studies field tends to be complex, the teacher has the responsibility of adjusting length of assignment to the type of reading required by the assignment. For example, if the teacher has in mind a general overview of a particular section, that purpose should be made clear with the added advice—"Read this rapidly to find out what it is about." On the other hand, if the purpose is the ability to follow a sequence of events in accurate chrono-logical steps the assignment should include—"Read this care-fully. Make notes or a simple outline of each event in the order in which it occurred." This procedure will do much to facilitate reading in the social studies.

Summary

The field of social studies requires a greater amount of reading than other subject areas because most of the knowl-edge of social studies must be acquired vicariously and be-cause the content of social studies is a rapidly expanding one. Social studies reading is difficult—it requires understanding of its own specialized vocabulary and the specific connota-tions of general vocabulary used in social studies context; it demands holding in mind many strands of simultaneous development in an organized relationship; it calls for critical thinking about basic issues; it forces the seeking of additional information for full understanding of many topics; it includes the ability to separate fact and opinion as well as to assess the value of each.

The social studies teacher who accepts the responsibility of making reading an integral part of the social studies pro-gram not only will increase competency in the acquisition of social studies content but will also be adding to the reading skills needed in any kind of research. The ability to recog-nize main ideas and relevant details is a basic skill in under-standing the factual type of writing used in social studies material. The recognition of the appropriateness of speed to the kind of material to be read and the purpose for reading will increase the efficiency of the student's reading.

The final test of the efficiency in reading of a secondary student is his ability to summarize in a logically organized manner the main points of his reading and to relate these ideas to modern living.

Suggested Readings

Five Steps to Reading Success in Science, Social Studies, and Mathematics. New York: Metropolitan School Study Council, 1954.

KAY, SYLVIA C. *Reading Critically (In the Fields of Literature and History).* New York: Twayne Publishers, 1952.

LEARY, BERNICE E. "Meeting Specific Reading Problems in the Content Fields," *Reading in the High School and College.* 47th Yearbook, National Society for the Study of Education. Chicago: University of Chicago Press, 1948. Pp. 171–78.

PETERSON, ELEANOR. *Aspects of Readability in the Social Studies.* New York: Bureau of Publications, Teachers College, Columbia University, 1954.

SPEER, EUNICE H. "Library Resource Materials for Reading in Social Studies," *Materials for Reading.* Supplementary Educational Monographs, No. 86. Chicago: University of Chicago Press, 1957.

The Suggestion Box

Using one chapter of a social science text, list all the words that are clearly defined in context. Compare this list to those words which are introduced but not clearly defined.

In a faculty group or a study group, ask each member to write his definition of the word *democracy* or some similar abstract term. Compare these definitions. How much of the definition is denotation? connotation?

State a question and ask the students to use the textbook in locating the answer to the question. Observe the use of table of contents or index. Encourage skimming for the answer, and discuss the cues used when one skims for a definite purpose. Ask the student to read carefully for the answer, close the book, and answer the question *in his own words.*

Make a list of five questions, each of which can be answered only by consulting maps, tables, graphs, or other illustrations; do not give clues as to the location of the answers. Discuss the value of illustrative materials in the textbook.

When short-answer or essay examinations are returned to the students, ask several students to read their responses to selected questions to provide a point of comparison for other students' responses.

IX

Reading in Science

HIGH SCHOOL STUDENTS ARE BEING ENCOURAGED to include much science in their programs of study, partially because of the strong public interest engendered by modern nuclear discoveries and space developments, partially because there is a shortage of science personnel and a career in science is currently a promising one. If secondary schools are to have extensive science offerings, it is obvious that students must be prepared to read efficiently in the various scientific fields and that every teacher of high school science will be responsible for teaching the reading skills that are peculiar to and crucial in his field.

Demands on science teachers for reading instruction. Students entering high school differ widely in their ability to read informational materials. Some have skills equivalent to those of a capable adult reader; others are quite retarded and read at a level normal to an average fourth-grade pupil; the remaining students range in ability anywhere between

156

these two extremes. The teacher of general science, which is usually an introductory course required of all students, is confronted by numerous reading problems. Some of his pupils know how to study; others do not. Certain ones have genuine interest in the sciences and have acquired an excellent background for his course; many of their classmates have a modicum of science information and have little or no interest.

The teacher of general science needs, early in the school year, to take inventory of the study and reading skills of his students, as well as to ascertain their science background and interests. After analyzing the results of standardized reading tests, he should devise informal tests and check lists that will reveal what his pupils' study habits are, what science vocabulary they already know, and which areas of science have the greatest appeal for them. He will watch them as they silently read short excerpts from the textbook so as to gauge their rate of reading and note any obvious signs of reading difficulty, such as frowning over difficult words or a tendency to daydream after a vainly laborious attempt at the overly difficult material. A little oral reading will further reveal the reading needs of his students.

Students suspected of having difficulty with the general reading skills may be referred to the English teachers—if the school has the policy of leaving these skills to the English department and having every other teacher responsible for cultivating the reading skills particularly pertinent to his subject. It is certainly the definite responsibility of each science teacher to discuss with his classes the make-up of the textbook and manual used in his course so that they understand its scheme of organization and note the different kinds of study aids that they should capitalize on as they prepare their lessons. As the course proceeds, he should introduce all new technical vocabulary meaningfully and make sure that the students have a clear-cut purpose for every reading activity in which he has them participate. It is particularly important that he prepare his students to read and use formulas, equations, symbols, and tables which so often summarize the key ideas in science.

Each teacher in the more advanced phases of science taught at the secondary level has his own particular responsibilities for teaching his students to read materials in his field efficiently. The general science teacher may have done much to introduce the more basic concepts and vocabulary and to guide his students into effective study techniques; but there are always students who need further instruction in these aspects of a science course. In addition to this reinforcing type of reading instruction, he will have responsibilities especially pertinent to his own course—introducing additional vocabulary, a different textbook and manual with study aids and special features that his students must learn to use properly. He may require more reference work in the library than did the teacher of general science and he must make sure that his students know how to use the particular kinds of references that are appropriate to his course.

Demands of science reading on the students. Even the most capable reader will find that science reading is not easy. Much of it requires slow, careful perusal with painstaking attention to detail. The vocabulary is highly specialized and extensive in each branch of the sciences. Since a full understanding of concepts is dependent on a ready use of technical terms that really have meaning to the students, they must make an effort to master each new technical word or phrase as they meet it. Most modern textbooks in science offer definite help in understanding newly introduced vocabulary through the use of accompanying pictures or graphic aids, contextual clues, and a glossary. As has been said, the teacher is responsible for indicating the various study aids which his textbook affords and for helping the students to know how to make use of these aids. Aids which give help with vocabulary are especially important, since the science textbook is likely to provide definitions and illustrations of greater precision than the meanings given in many dictionaries.

A major difficulty in science reading is that some of the vocabulary and symbolization of mathematics is also used in scientific materials but the meanings are by no means identical. For instance, the meanings of terms such as *inversion, base, solution,* and *radical* in science must not be confused with mathematical connotations for these words. The "plus" symbol in *arithmetic* means that two numbers are to be combined into a total quantity; in *algebra* it designates a positive number; in *chemistry* the sign means neither of these, but rather symbolizes the idea of "reacts with." It is all too easy for an instructor to assume that the students are aware of such specialized meanings in his field of science; but this is an unwise assumption. Few students can meet the demands of a specialized vocabulary as they read unless the teacher gives special attention to important technical terms as they come up.

Students may similarly confuse their general and special social science vocabulary with that in their sciences. The term *culture* is a good illustration. Other multi-meaninged words that have an exact connotation in the sciences are *force, pressure, property, recoil, liberation, retort, reaction, gravity, density, friction,* and *circuit.* It is evident that the teacher must ever be on the alert for terms whose meanings in science differ from meanings already familiar but different and that he must be sure to guide his students to ensure correct impressions.

The demands of specialized vocabulary, however, are but one of the problems to be met if the students are to read efficiently. Passages within a textbook may vary widely in difficulty; for example, these passages that deal with light.[1]

The people of ancient times were sun worshippers. Light represented good to them, while darkness represented evil. Since the moon and stars gave off light, they also held these heavenly bodies in awe.

Early man had to stay at home most nights because he had no way to see in the dark.

But note the subsequent passage:

We get heat and light from the sun. But how do they reach us? It cannot be by conduction, since there is little matter between us and the sun. And the sun is 93 million miles away! It cannot be by convection either, since there is no matter to circulate.

Heat and light from the sun reach us by *radiation.* Radiation, in the form of vibrations or ripples, spreads through space in all directions especially noticeable from any hot or lighted body. When the vibrations strike the earth's surface or any object, they set the molecules they touch into more rapid vibration, thus giving them heat. Some of these radiations affect the eye, and we call them light.

The students will probably have no difficulty in under-

[1] Ira C. Davis, John Burnett, and E. Wayne Gross, *Science Discovery and Progress* (New York: Henry Holt and Co., 1957), p. 241.

standing the first of these two excerpts; but the more technical language and difficult style of expression in the second
one call for a much greater degree of concentration and more
exact knowledge of words.

However, the real demand on the reading of students lies
in their ability to read a number of related passages and to
determine the main idea and relate to it the major supporting
details. The main idea in the passages above is that heat and
light reach the earth through radiation. In arriving at this
conclusion students must use the information that neither
conduction nor convection, because of the lack of matter
between the earth and the sun, can account for light and
heat; that radiation spreads through space and strikes the
earth's surface; that the ripples of radiation set molecules on
the earth's surface into rapid vibration and, in the process,
release heat.

Here, within one short section of the book, the student is
required to recall what is meant by *conduction* and *convection* and to learn the new concept of *radiation*. In addition
he gets an initial idea of the difference between *heat waves*
and *light waves*. This concise statement of the several facts
seems deceptively simple but is truly complex; it is typical
of the idea-packed materials that students find in their
science books. The reading demands on students are indeed
heavy, as sentence after sentence, paragraph after paragraph,
and page after page they must "work" their way through
science textbooks. If they learn to ferret out main ideas and
select related details that give the central thought meaning
and substance they will have met one of the heaviest demands of science reading.

Helping students to read science materials efficiently. The responsibility of the science teacher to introduce the students to his textbook and to acquaint them with the study helps has already been discussed. Next will be suggested some ways for him to help students master the technical vocabulary that is basic to understanding science materials.

At the beginning of the course the instructor should indicate how important the vocabulary of science is and should suggest ways of acquiring it. He should then consistently take time to teach new words and expressions directly; for instance, he might say: "Have you heard the word *frequency* before? What does it mean? Now skim the second paragraph on page 49 and find the word *frequency*. See if you can make a good guess on what the word means in this paragraph." Afterward he would lead a clarifying discussion of the new meaning.

Often it is advisable for the science teacher to write particularly important new terms on the chalkboard or to make a chart on which all the new technical terms in a particular science section are listed. As each of these words is taken up, it should be pronounced, located in the textbook so that the contextual clues in the passage may be located to clarify the concept, and the excerpt should be talked over so as to guarantee meaningful learning.

Note this illustrative treatment of excerpts from a chemistry textbook:

What is valence? It would be rather awkward for chemists to talk about the "combining capacity" of an element. Instead, they have coined a special, shorter word which means "combining capacity." That word is *valence.*[2]

[2] Charles E. Dull, H. Clark Metcalfe, and John E. Williams, *Modern Chemistry* (New York: Henry Holt and Co., 1958), p. 66.

Immediately following this simple definition there is a technical discussion of types of chemical bonding. Finally in italics appears the statement:

Valence is the number of electrons which an atom gains, loses, or shares in bonding with one or more atoms.[3]

In dealing with new concepts, the teacher writes *valence* on the chalkboard, pronounces it, and has the students turn to the proper page in the textbook to locate the term, to think through the passages which describe the concept and give a final definition, to note the contextual clues, and to be ready with questions about any still-obscure meaning. Such treatment impresses on the students the fact that here are a basic concept and an important definition that must be understood and mastered, if they are to understand later references in the textbook and solve prospective problems on valence.

Another way of assisting students to acquire vocabulary and gain clear concepts is by calling attention to frequently recurring prefixes, roots, and suffixes, so abundant in science terms. When the word *transparent* is first taken up as a scientific term, the prefix *trans* should be dealt with. Then when *translucent* appears in a passage the students will be partially ready to understand it. In conjunction with the information that *luc* refers to light, the knowledge of *trans* helps to make the second new word meaningful. If students combine their knowledge of word parts with contextual clues they are likely to read with understanding.

Steps in carrying out an experiment are details. The student must consider steps as such as he reads in his manual. If a student can be trained to think of the general purpose

[3] *Ibid.,* p. 71.

of an experiment as the main idea (What will this experiment prove?) and the steps in carrying out the experiment as the details (What are the materials and the steps?) he will be able to economize on time and be more successful in getting satisfactory results. For example, if he is to experiment to find out how soap and detergents affect hard water, he might be asked to follow the directions below:

Finding the Effects of Soap on Hard Water

Compare what happens when you add soap to soft water (distilled water) and to hard water (limewater). Fill a test tube one-third full of distilled water and to this add 5 drops of liquid soap. Shake it to form suds. To the test tube which is one-third full of limewater add 5 drops of liquid soap and shake the tube vigorously. Let this tube stand for a minute or so and observe what happens.

For further experimentation take another test tube one-third full of distilled water and add a pinch of Epsom salts. Again add 5 drops of liquid soap and shake vigorously. How does the second type of distilled water with the salts differ from the others?

Clearly the main idea of this experimentation is to make a comparison of the actions of soap on hard and on soft water. The details consist of the step-by-step use of materials in performing the experiment. If a student learns to read experiments with the main idea in mind and to arrange the details under suitable headings (three probably) he has simplified his assignment considerably.

Materials   What to do   Observations of what happened

Sequence in a cycle is another example of a *main idea* and the *details*. In learning what is meant by a complete meta-morphosis the student should think of the details as the different appearances at each stage of development and the characteristics of each change.

A final reading skill which the science student should utilize is that of relating what he reads to his own experiences. The instructor should point out to the class that all around in home and community are numerous examples of scientific principles in operation. If the student learns to recall familiar practical applications for highly abstract science ideas as he reads he will add greatly to his powers of comprehension and not rely on meaningless memorization of facts as a mode of learning. For example, *air pressure* should be related to such everyday experiences as operation of bicycle pumps, drinking through a straw, medicine droppers, and siphons.

Notes and outlines are valuable study helps to science students (see Chapter VII, "How to Study in Every Subject") especially for review purposes. Summaries and review questions also are important items for reviewing and self-testing. If the science student can learn system as he studies, is consistent in his habits of reading, and adjusts his speed to the type of material he has won half the battle of achieving success in science.

Summary

The rapid changes in our world due to advancement in scientific knowledge and the consequent increasing demand for scientists and technicians are increasing the enrollment in science courses. No matter how enthusiastic the students may be, unless they can read science material with understanding and with ease they are going to be handicapped in their progress.

The reading of science material calls for skill in adjusting to various types of written presentation, in the mastering of a technical vocabulary, in differentiating meanings of words and symbols as used in science and other content subjects, and in building science concepts through selection of main idea and related details. Much of science reading must be slow, careful reading. Following a consistent, effective method of reading and study will be one way the student can build toward success in science.

Suggested Readings

AUSTRHEIM, BERNICE. "Materials for the Unit Plan—In Science," *Materials for Reading.* Supplementary Educational Monographs, No. 86. Chicago: University of Chicago Press, 1957. Pp. 162–66.

BROWN, CLYDE M. "Reading in Science as a Means of Improving the Junior High School Program," *Science Teacher,* XXI (November, 1954), 281–83.

MALLISON, GEORGE G. "How to Use the Textbook in Science Teaching," *School Science and Mathematics,* LIII (November, 1953), 593–600.

McCALLISTER, JAMES M. "Aspects of Books That Affect Readability in Science," *Materials for Reading.* Supplementary Educational Monographs, No. 86, Chicago: University of Chicago Press, 1957. Pp. 174–78.

VAN DEVENTER, WILLIAM C. "Library Resource Materials for Reading—In Science," *Materials for Reading.* Supplementary Educational Monographs, No. 86. Chicago: University of Chicago Press, 1957. Pp. 186–90.

The Suggestion Box

Select a scientific term, such as *hemiptera*. Ask the students to study its root and discuss its origin (*pteron*, from the Greek). Encourage a search of the text and supplementary materials for other examples of this particular root as it is applied to scientific terminology.

Encourage a week's search of magazines and newspapers for articles on a topic discussed in class and taken from the textbook.

In a laboratory science, direct the students to read carefully the instructions for an experiment. Encourage them to visualize each step, even to the selection of equipment. Discuss the experiment step by step, including location and use of equipment and materials. After the experiment, discuss the value of knowing the details of directions before beginning a task.

Encourage reports on scientific fiction. Discuss the use of scientific facts and principles in the development of the story. In what way did the author depart from truth in order to present an entertaining story?

Select a section of the textbook which is written in simple expository form but shifts abruptly to compact presentation of data. Ask students to read this selection and to discuss changes which occurred in their reading patterns.

X

Reading in English

To the english teacher has fallen the task of teaching whatever reading is taught in most of our secondary schools. The assumption on the part of most of the other teachers in the school that the English teacher can and will teach the necessary skills is, of course, a false one. As a matter of fact, many English teachers are not really prepared to do a good job of teaching reading, even in their own area of literature. The teacher of English is quite often a person who has read well all of his school life; he has appreciated good literature; he has developed refined tastes and intense interests; he has regarded the reading of literature as a matter of second nature. He has been attracted to the teaching of English because he has always enjoyed reading.

This same person frequently does not have an understanding of the difficulties that many young people encounter when they attempt to read poetry, the essay, or the novel.

168

He is often neither tolerant nor patient with the student who simply has never been interested in reading for appreciation of good literature.

We no longer subscribe to the tenets of formal discipline that the reading of good literature "improves the mind" or "disciplines thinking" so that there will be transfer of this ability to other subject areas. Instead, we believe that the following clear-cut purposes should be attained through reading literature—whether fictional or informational:

1. Good literature can and should enrich personal living. We are quite definitely, as a society, moving toward a shorter working day and a minimum working week. Never before have young people and adults had so much leisure time. If we believe that the reading of literature can fill personal needs in the individual, then we see it as a more-than-adequate competitor for television, radio, movies, spectator sports, and do-it-yourself hobbies.

2. We read to secure facts about subjects that interest us. Here, the skills of reference are needed—where to look, how to find it, and what to do with it after we get it.

3. We read to learn how to do something. An examination of popular family magazines demonstrates that editors are quite aware of the mass appeal of the article which informs readers how to decorate a home, plan a garden, cook a tasty dish, or mend a crumbling wall.

4. Much of our reading is directed toward questioning hypotheses. The intellectually curious student finds this type of reading challenging; the dull must be led gently into simpler challenging materials.

5. We read to verify an opinion, to substantiate a fact.

6. We read to gain a general impression: What is this novel about? Does it have appeal for me? Is the author's style familiar, unique, effective?

7. We read to solve a problem. In the area of literature, this

so often depends upon the ability of the reader to identify with a character in fiction or history and to learn how that character solved his problems. Young people gain support and solace from reading of the lives of great men and women and discerning that they, too, had problems similar to their own.

8. We read to understand and to gain appreciation for a general theme, an idea, or a principle.

The teacher's role. Prerequisite to the teacher's ability to teach reading skills and to develop appreciation in the student is his own ability to read with skill and pleasure. Effective indeed is the teacher who reads aloud in order to share a thing of beauty which has stirred him deeply.

More than ever before, a student has the opportunity to read widely according to his personal tastes. The teacher no longer depends upon prescribed reading lists. There is an abundance of books—good books—written at every level of difficulty and designed to suit every interest and taste. But because many young people simply do not know how to locate what they want to read, sending them to the library is not the complete answer. Interests are aroused and heightened by a good teacher's example, by his frequent references to challenging, thought- and interest-provoking books, periodicals, and articles.

Fresh from his university training in literature, the beginning English teacher may regard with dismay his students' choices of books. He has been cautioned, perhaps, that he should disdain Zane Grey and Jack London. But how often a young student's interests, fanned to a flame by such an author as London, has been tactfully transferred by a sympathetic and understanding, experienced teacher to *Gulliver's*

Travels or *Moby Dick!* Unfortunately, there has crept into the teaching of much of our literature a preoccupation with books of the here-and-now. No one will deny the value of *Kon-Tiki, Annapurna,* or *The Old Man and the Sea;* but the student who finds these titles interesting deserves a diet balanced with *The Ordeal of Richard Feverel, Les Miserables,* and *The Return of the Native.*

The teacher of English will give young people many opportunities to share their reading, to share freely their enthusiasm for the recently finished novel or short story. He will identify the student who responds to poetry and surround him with anthologies of modern and classical poems. He will provide periods during which his students feel free to use each other as sounding boards for their ideas and their enthusiasms.

An error in judgment is frequently made when we assume that students who read well, from a skills-development standpoint, are also capable of reacting to and interpreting what they read. Many excellent readers lack the experiences to understand and react to the novel; on the other hand, we frequently find students who, though they read laboriously, bring to the page a wealth of personal experience and are adequate in their interpretation and reaction. This latter group can give support to the able but experience-limited reader, just as the able reader can often guide the plodder toward more adequate skills development. High school youth are quick to follow the example of others.

The teacher's role is to guide, by example and by direct teaching, in order that young men and women may be led to higher and more mature levels of reading, wherein they will develop not only an appreciation for literary merit but also a respect for the personal and social values that are often reflected in our heritage of good literature.

Poetry

It seems apparent that the first step in leading students toward enjoyment of poetry is the development of an awareness of poetry as spoken language. The ability to read and enjoy poetry depends not only upon the reader's awareness of pattern of organization, imagery, figurative language, obscure themes, and emotional intent but upon a real familiarity with each of these; hence, direct teaching is demanded.

If students are to recognize and to appreciate the intricacies of poetry they must hear much reading of simple poetry so that they may develop good listening skills. As they find poems of strong appeal they should carefully prepare to read them aloud to their classmates. They may use poems collected from many sources—magazines, textbooks, anthologies. A technique used widely in the elementary school, that of choral reading of poetry, is even more suited to use in secondary English classes. The magnificent effects obtained from group reading of simple poetry have often awakened deep and abiding interest in students who otherwise had never enjoyed a poem.

So much enthusiasm for good poetry has been killed by attempting to launch a unit based on seventeenth- and eighteenth-century poets upon students who do not have the maturity for understanding sophisticated poetry. That our students will come to understand and appreciate classical poetry may be an ultimate aim in the teaching of English to the more advanced students; but we cannot begin with classical poems that are obscure in theme, distorted in word order, or vague in their symbolism. A carefully laid foundation of Carl Sandburg, Robert Frost (yes, Ogden Nash!), or William Rose Benét may make it possible to build for a subsequent enjoyment of Chaucer and Shakespeare.

The reading of poetry demands an ability to recall and again feel vicariously sense impressions, a skill that grows gradually with much hearing of poetry. Again, we should make a cautious and careful beginning with simple and easily apparent sensory impressions:

> When men were all asleep the snow came flying,
> In large white flakes falling on the city brown,
> Stealthily and perpetually settling and loosely lying
> Hushing the latest traffic of the drowsy town.
> "London Snow" by ROBERT BRIDGES (1844–1930)

In contrast to the simplicity of the sense impressions awakened by these lines are those of Michael Drayton, from "Poly-Olbion, The Thirteenth Song" (1612):

> To forests that belongs, but yet this is not all:
> With solitude what sorts that here's not wondrous rife?
> Whereas the hermit leads a sweet retired life
> From villages replete with ragg'd and sweating clowns,
> And from the loathsome airs of smoky citied towns.

Here we have lines suited to only the sophisticated and intellectually mature lovers of poetry.

Simile, metaphor, alliteration, rhyme, rhythm, onomatopoeia—this is the vocabulary of poetry; poetry that takes on meaning as innumerable and progressively more subtle poems are read and enjoyed. None of the specialized characteristics of poetry will be valued and appreciated by the student unless they afford pleasure through his being able to understand and react pleasurably to what he hears or reads to others. The goal is not a scholarly knowledge of the intricacies of poetry but a deep and lasting appreciation for the ideas of the poem itself that is artistically expressed. The inexperienced teacher, lover of poetry and literary critic though he may be, should guard carefully against his tendencies to overinterpret simple poetry. Scholarly dissection has often killed a lovely poem for a group of pupils who should listen for pure enjoyment.

One final word: A major hurdle in the reading of poetry is the subordination of a clearly stated rhythm to the meaning. The child is accustomed to and fascinated by the singsong rhythm of the nursery rhyme, and we frequently find a high school student who ignores meaning and surrenders himself to a strict observance of rhythm. Rhythm is but one facet of the poem—usually not too significant—but to subordinate it is oftentimes difficult for the pattern-conscious student. He must learn first to seek meaning and mood. Observe the distortion of meaning which results from dependence upon rhythm in reading this quotation from Whittier's familiar "Snowbound":

> A prompt, decisive man, no breath
> Our father wasted "Boys, a path!"

A high school student puzzled for years over the fact that "Boys, a path!" was wasted!

The Novel

Our boys and girls are living in a society whose speedy tempo is reflected in programs of television, the movie, and radio. Plots are launched and action is introduced with little verbiage. The plot of a 500-page book is reduced to a one-hour televised performance; the senses of our students are keyed to a rapid pace, and the first four chapters of the nineteenth-century novel may fail to take them anywhere. Consider, for a moment, this opening paragraph of *Bleak House:*

London. Michaelmas Term lately over, and the Lord Chancellor sitting in Lincoln's Inn Hall. Implacable November weather. As much mud in the streets, as if the waters had but newly retired from the face of the earth, and it would not be wonderful to meet a Megalosaurus, forty feet long or so, waddling like an elephantine lizard up Holborn Hill. Smoke lowering down from chimney-pots, making a soft black drizzle, with flakes of soot in it as big as full-grown snow-flakes—gone mourning, one might imagine, for the death of the sun. Dogs, undistinguishable in mire. Horses, scarcely better; splashed to their very blinkers. Foot passengers, jostling one another's umbrellas, in a general infection of ill-temper, and losing their foot-hold at street-corners, where tens of thousands of other foot passengers have been slipping and sliding since the day broke (if this day ever broke), adding new deposits to the crust upon crust of mud, sticking at those points tenaciously to the pavement, and accumulating at compound interest. CHARLES DICKENS, 1852.

To the mature, experienced reader, such a paragraph may be both interesting and tantalizing; the appeal to the senses is great, and the stage is carefully and painstakingly set. On the other hand, the student who has had little experience in reading Dickens and comparable authors may decide, after a few paragraphs, that the story simply isn't "going anywhere." Attuned to the pace of the modern "slick" and the paperback thriller, this student may turn away from Dickens with disgust.

Herein lies the challenge to the teacher! To aid students in establishing habits of reading good literature the teacher must start where his students are. He may have to adjust his personal tastes and select more modern, fast-moving fiction. He can capture the interest of the students with one of the many good juvenile books which are available in quantities and which do not actually represent subliterary standards of writing. Obviously we do not believe that juvenile literature should be accepted as standard fare throughout the years of secondary school training. But the student who reads *Treasure Island* with relish can gradually grow in reading power so that he can pleasurably tackle another great sea story, *Moby Dick*.

Nothing gains more from uninterrupted reading than does the novel; nothing gains less from analytical, intensive study. The able reader of the novel may, if he likes, skim like the wind over involved description, or immerse himself deeply in the passage that strikes a sympathetic chord, or linger thoughtfully over a few sentences which created a unique picture of extraordinary appeal. He identifies characters and sets them in perspective of place and time and situation; he sees and follows involved relationships and sequences. He anticipates action, and thrills at a climax.

At the secondary school level it would seem inadvisable ever to teach a novel for its form, except to the extent that form is necessary for understanding the message of the novel. Critical analysis is seldom warranted in other than college-preparatory classes. Even with the college-bound student there is always the danger of robbing him of the pleasure that he might derive from reading the novel as he chooses, when he chooses.

This is not to say that the teacher has no responsibility for teaching students how to read a book. Frequent discussions, oral reports, and total-group examination of the good novel are desirable, if students' needs and purposes are recognized and not forced into a rigid pattern or set response.

The teacher of English, working daily with students of all levels of ability and interest, will soon discover that few students read a specific novel at exactly the same depth of comprehension. As an example of the various depths at which a heterogeneous group of students—heterogeneous in terms of ability, interests, experiences, and sex—might respond to a novel, let us take Hardy's *Return of the Native:*

1. To the inexperienced and immature reader, this novel will present nothing more than a simple story of simple people, in a remote area of England. The characters will appear to be either "bad" or "good" as exemplified by Eustacia and Thomasin, for example.
2. At the next level, this is a story of the complicated relationships of people who are bound together by their being compelled to live on Egdon Heath. They become victims of their own weaknesses and their inability to escape their environment.
3. At a sophisticated level, this is a "high" tragedy; the reader detects that Egdon Heath is an agent of destiny. It is symbolic of a time to come when "human souls may find themselves in closer and closer harmony with external things wearing a somberness distasteful to our race when it was young." Eustacia Vye becomes one of the greatest characters in fiction: lustful, prayerful, lovable, hateful. The reader detects the message of the author, even though Hardy injects little explanation or analysis. Doom hovers throughout the novel; mankind cannot escape nature, nor the inhumanity of man to man.

Obviously these are but three of many possible interpretations of this novel. It is important that the teacher recognize that varying depths of reading are to be expected of a group of students; equal in importance is his acceptance of these interpretations, without attempting to force a single interpretation upon the group. His task, rather, is to encourage and to aid students in detecting and appreciating the message of the novel, at a depth appropriate to their current stage of advancement.

Here are a few suggestions which the teacher might find helpful in his attempts to encourage his students to read good books:

1. Seize every opportunity to "sell" a book to the students. Carry armloads of books into the classroom, discuss each one briefly, and allow each student to select the one he would like to read.

2. Occasionally select books for those students whom you know so as to widen their range of choice and to keep them "growing" in taste. Let them know that you have confidence in their ability and their interest by encouraging them to read the book and discuss it with you.

3. Watch for television and movie presentations of standard novels. Hold discussions of the forthcoming production and set guidelines for viewing and listening. Set aside a class period for discussion and critical analysis of the production.

4. Encourage good readers to present panel discussions of the books they have read. The student who does not read well may be encouraged to read a book if it is presented with interest and enthusiasm by a person whom he respects and admires.

5. Allow your students to select books for themselves; although we are interested in improving interests and tastes, we must realize that a positive beginning must be made.

The present interest of the student must be recognized; deeper, more acceptable interest may later result if we accept the student's momentary desire to read a book which we do not consider "good" literature and do not alienate him by ridiculing or forbidding him to follow his current interest.

6. Challenge students to write brief reports on books they have read, and keep those reports on file where other students may read them; the good report is likely to lead another student to read the book.

7. Occasionally read a novel aloud to a group of students. Allow discussion at the end of each reading, but do not demand detailed analysis.

8. Set up groups of students, with each group reading a single title. Ask the group to select one person to report the book to the rest of the class.

9. Occasionally set aside a period for free reading, either in the classroom or in the library. Allow students to feel that they do not have to report this reading, if they choose not to report.

10. Encourage your students to read professional book reviews in periodicals and newspapers, to use these reviews as guides in their own selection, and to share their reviews with other members of the class.

11. As a substitute for the standard book list, encourage students to prepare annotations of books. A book will be placed on the class list of suggested titles only if it receives at least three favorable responses from the students.

Biography

Frequently the secondary school teacher of English complains that his students have lost interest in biography—an interest which most students have had during early adolescence as they yearned for identification with historical heroes and heroines; then they read biographies with gusto. Biographies should have great appeal to students throughout the secondary school, but the interest in a particular biography is often something not shared by another student. Consequently, it is difficult to use the biography for common reading in a class. Also, biographies of scientists and statesmen may require knowledge of background which is much too complex for the average student. On the other hand, the characters in a biography really do or did live, and some students will react more positively to the reality in the life of a great person than they will to the fictional character in a novel.

An interest in biography is often heightened as an awareness is developed of its form and the intent of the author. A helpful classification of the biography is this one, which divides biographies into three types:

1. The "monument" type, which extols the virtues of the man and perceives him as a triumph of perfection.
2. The "document" type, which is a statement of facts and chronology and may or may not praise the man.
3. The "gargoyle" type, which casts the man with clay feet, attempts to debunk previous accounts of his virtues and deeds, and frequently maligns.

The student may through rapid skimming be led to discover the type of biography he is reading. He should attempt to discover the purpose or intent of the writer. Extremely important is the relationship of the writer to the subject; if he is a member of the subject's family he may not be capable of objectivity in presenting the subject's life. On the other hand, if he has not done a thorough research on the life of the subject, his presentation may be grossly inaccurate. Students should be encouraged to read another biography of the same subject and compare the authors' presentations of the essential facts.

Disheartening to some students is the realization that many of the characters and events in a biography are fictionalized, whereas they originally believed that all the ideas and events were real. The teacher should help the student to see that writers often attempt to create a semblance of authenticity through the use of fictional characters and events which are used to delineate the events of the subject's life.

To develop interest in biography, the teacher may choose to use some of these suggestions:

1. Select contemporary figures and discuss their contributions; these may be sports figures or people in entertainment, politics, or education. Collect as many facts as possible about these people; compare these contemporary people and their lives to those of historical figures. Several students will be encouraged to read biography in order to obtain the desired information.
2. Encourage groups of students to write, direct, and present a program similar to the "This Is Your Life" episodes, basing their information on the reading of selected biographies.
3. Select a biography for class reading and discussion. Follow this activity by careful research in the library to test the authenticity of the biography.
4. Encourage the students to read several biographies about a single person. The biographies of George Washington Carver, Franklin D. Roosevelt, and Emily Dickinson are particularly fruitful for this purpose.

The Short Story

The short story is one of the most popular literary forms in high school English classes. Nearly everyone loves a good story, and the range of short stories available to the student is wide. Students who cannot be convinced of the value of the novel may be encouraged to read good short stories; and, actually, if they become really interested in the short story they can be led frequently to the reading of novels.

Short stories are usually of three easily recognized types:

1. The story of character. The character may be revealed through action, characteristic details, conversation, dialect, or characteristic language.
2. The story of theme. This type of short story depends heavily upon the reader's ability to infer motives, social significance, feelings or moods, or significance of a particular event.
3. The story of situation. In this type characters are subordinated to a particular setting or episode. The characters are generally victims of, or controlled by, the situation.

Although magazines are the most common source of short stories, one should not overlook the value of the many excellent anthologies available for classroom use. The teacher may gain valuable information concerning the level of stories which are read by his students if he asks them to list the magazines they prefer to read. There are three commonly accepted classifications of periodicals which indicate the level of the student's reading:

1. Level 1: *The New Yorker, Harper's, The Atlantic Monthly.*
2. Level 2: *The Saturday Evening Post, Redbook, Good Housekeeping.*
3. Level 3: Those periodicals which are referred to as "pulps" and "slicks"—romances, confessions, westerns, for instance.

To aid the student in learning to read the short story for appreciation and interpretation the teacher may use these suggestions:

1. Read for stereotypes in character development. Are terms such as *hillbilly, teen-ager, glamour girl,* and *inspector* overworked and misleading?
2. Read for awareness of the form of the story. A common form is that of the "flash-back," in which a situation is presented at a climax and the action moves backward for clarification of events which led to the climax. Another popular form employs the surprise ending; perhaps the most difficult form is that of the logical sequence culminating in an implied climax which allows the reader to infer his own choice in resolving the plot.
3. Select a short story for dramatization; assign a group of students to the task of writing the play.
4. Give opportunities for students to read short stories aloud to the group. This provides an excellent means of comparing the literary merits of the stories. Discussion should bring out the fact that one can usually predict the outcome of a short story which appears in the Level 3 category (see above), while those stories which are published in Level 1 periodicals are usually much more unpredictable and sophisticated and possess greater literary merit.

Drama

While reading the drama can be extremely entertaining, no type of literature requires more of the reader. He must be, first of all, capable of listening or reading carefully and critically. Much must be "read between the lines." In a good play there is no unnecessary conversation; a single phrase may convey subtle meanings.

The student who reads drama must visualize not only the details of the setting but the action, the characters, and numerous implied events. If he is watching a performance he must constantly feel the relationship of music and poetry to the drama.

It is always advisable to read a few plays for the understanding of the characters only, a few for the understanding of plot only, and a few for the visualization of staging. Many students are confused if we demand that they see the play in its entirety; many good dramas are written in such a way that action is implied by a single line which sets the stage for the entire play. Consequently, it is best that the reading of plays proceed slowly until the student is experienced in mentally re-creating the characters, understanding plot, and visualizing settings simultaneously.

The reading of plays should proceed more slowly and carefully than the reading of the short story or the novel. Particular emphasis should be placed upon the first scenes; these often set the situation for the entire play. Also, a number of plays which contain symbolism may be too difficult for the inexperienced reader. It would be best to start with the simple plot and the uncomplicated setting and character development; *Everyman* and *The Rivals* cannot be appreciated by students who have not first learned the techniques of reading simple plays.

The best experience that can be provided for the student in learning to appreciate and interpret plays is that of reading orally the various parts. This can be accomplished as students work in small groups, with members of each group exchanging roles occasionally; or, parts can be assigned to certain students in the class, and the members of the class may act as critics in terms of the interpretation of the characters which is given by the readers.

Drama mirrors the life and times of which it is a part. It is not a simple glass into which a student can look casually. The skills of reading dramatic literature are complex; but the truths of human experience a student will find—when he is capable of looking purposefully, intelligently, and penetratingly into the mirror—are well worth the combined efforts of the teacher and the student. Once the skills are mastered the student has a new tool, his personal mirror of life, through which he can know himself.[1]

The Essay

The essay demands more complex skill of the reader, for it may present a detailed expansion of a single idea, bit of information, or opinion which the author desires to express. He may write seriously; he may employ tongue-in-cheek whimsy; or he may cloak his message in allegory. Whatever his vehicle, his purpose for writing the essay must be deduced. Therein lies the difficulty for the reader. Many of the essays recommended for reading in the secondary school are simply too difficult for the average student, particularly the works of Macaulay, Huxley, and similar writers. Robert Benchley and James Thurber, on the other hand, are essayists whose works are both entertaining and enlightening; their essays may be read widely by secondary school students.

Possibly the most important skill demanded for a student's intelligent reading of an essay is that of logical thinking; he must be able to recognize patterns of organization and to weigh each idea carefully in terms of the author's purpose. With practice, the student may be led to discover whether the author reveals himself or remains an impersonal dispenser of ideas or information. Since the essay is usually short, careful reading of each word and each sentence is required. No

[1] Dwight L. Burton, *Literature Study in the High Schools* (New York: Henry Holt and Co., 1959), p. 216.

other form of literature demands more deliberate concentration or more careful analysis.

Summary

No teacher in the high school has a richer opportunity to aid young people in the development of personal reading interests and tastes than does the English teacher. Our heritage of literature offers something for every young person, regardless of his ability, his previous experiences, or his interests. But the English teacher cannot assume that literature will immediately be of equal value to all students, nor can he assume that all students are capable of reading every assignment. Special skills are demanded for the reading of all types of literature, and the development of those skills must go hand in hand with the daily assignments. The awakening of the desire to read and to share good literature and to make the reading of good books, poetry, essays, and drama a lifelong source of satisfaction for our students constitutes the most challenging task of the teacher of English.

Suggested Readings

BURTON, DWIGHT L. *Literature Study in the High Schools.* New York: Henry Holt and Co., 1959.

FRIEDRICH, GERHARD. "A Teaching Approach to Poetry," *The English Journal,* XLIX (February, 1960), 75–81.

GROMMON, ALFRED H. "Who Is 'The Leader of the People'? Helping Students Examine Fiction," *The English Journal,* XLVIII (November, 1959), 449–61.

GUNN, M. AGNELLA. "What Does Research in Reading Tell the Teacher of English in the Secondary School?" *What We Know about High School Reading.* Champaign, Ill.: National Council of Teachers of English, 1957–58. Pp. 3–6.

LAIRD, HELENE, and LAIRD, CHARLTON. *The Tree of Language.* Cleveland: World Publishing Co., 1957.

The Suggestion Box

Consult M. Newton Friend's *Words: Tricks and Traditions* (Scribner's, 1957) for word games, boners, limericks, puzzles, etc.

Compile a list of authorities and their fields of specialization (for example, Rachel Carson—oceanography; Luther Burbank—plant life; Wernher von Braun—guided missiles), placing the names in one column and the specializations in another column. Ask students to match authority and specialization; discuss the importance of knowing the background of an author in order to select the most reliable data.

As a means of emphasizing oral reading, tape-record the reading of a poem or piece of prose by several students. In another class, where the voices will not be recognized, discuss the relative merits of the readers.

Collect book jackets and compare the "blurbs" on the jackets with the criticism of the book by a student who has read it.

For the more able students, organize a club for the critical review of current fiction. Encourage individual reactions, but insist upon defense of viewpoint.

XI

Reading in Mathematics

WHEN THE AUTHORS OF *What Shall the High Schools Teach* [1] described the reading problem in the content fields by stating that each separate field has its own symbols and formulas, its own technical terminologies and special vocabularies, they accurately described reading in the various branches of mathematics. Any mathematics textbook, no matter how thoughtfully written, makes heavy demands on the student's reading ability. Teachers in this area have an inescapable responsibility for developing their students' reading skills in relationship to mathematical material if successful work in mathematics is to be attained. The student must follow steps in a process; interpret accurately mathematical vocabulary; recognize numerous abbreviations; approximate meanings of words through a knowledge of prefixes, suffixes, and roots; recognize the continuity of ideas from arithmetic through algebra, geometry, and higher mathematics; grasp concepts so that the structure of

[1] ASCD Yearbook, 1956, p. 186.

188

mathematics becomes of even greater importance than the processes.

The newer mathematics texts have considered the developmental level of the students who will be using the book. The material is organized to guide students into good study habits; to provide them maintenance and review exercises; to serve as a teacher when the student is working independently. For example, in a general mathematics text the authors state in the preface:

Whenever they are useful, boxed examples illustrate correct procedures to be practiced, reducing the amount of explanation required from the teacher, and serving as a convenient reference for the student.[2]

Introducing the textbook to the students. When students begin work with a new textbook the instructor will find that having the students examine the book under his direction and questioning is eventually one of the most valuable instructions he gives to his class. Getting an overview of the contents; learning that there are general as well as specific study helps; finding out how new mathematical vocabulary is introduced; locating informational sections; discovering that familiar objects and situations are used to connect the mathematical learning with its everyday applications; and knowing that there is a glossary that gives precise definitions give the student a sense of security and a feeling that the textbook is his most valuable resource because it is always available.

Expectations of students' reading. Some mention of the heavy demands of mathematical textbooks in students' read-

---

[2] Lucien B. Kinney, Vincent Ruble, and M. Russell Blythe, *General Mathematics* (New York: Henry Holt and Co., 1960), p. vi.

ing has been made in preceding sections. Here a more detailed account will be given.

It is, of course, essential that high school students have adequate general reading abilities if they are to interpret mathematical language. They must, for instance, have mastered the essential word-recognition skills, have learned to use contextual clues readily, have proficiency in applying prefixes, suffixes, and roots to new words; have become skillful in following a pattern of ideas, of recognizing main ideas and the required details; and have developed considerable skill in efficient use of the textbook.

For instance, they should habitually use the index for quick location of a topic; the glossary for the definition of a term; topical headings as leads into the ideas to be stressed in a subsection of a chapter; graphs, charts, and diagrams as vehicles for conveying comparative data.

Lack of general reading ability should be reported to the counselor or other responsible faculty member so that students may be assigned either to a special reading class or for specific help in an English class.

However, certain reading abilities must be stressed in the individual mathematics classes. For example, the mathematics teacher can be of great help in pointing out to students the intense concentration that reading in mathematics demands. Another important aspect of mathematical reading is its symbolic, abstract nature. Signs, symbols, and formulas that involve relationships carry so many ideas that this type of reading must be developed to the point where it is as easily read and interpreted as verbal passages. The skills involved in these types of reading are the important carry-overs into adult life—studying tax tables, hospitalization plans, insurance reports, the stock market, distribution of the tax dollar, and population trends. Graphs, pictographs, schedules, time-tables, and diagrams are parts of the information all literate people need.

Another factor in reading mathematics is the nature of the material. The student may have been hearing in other classes about the desirability of increasing reading speed. In reading mathematics he must be encouraged to use slow, careful reading. A look at the brevity of each individual problem should convince the student that there are few wasted words. No part can be skimmed lightly; rereading is frequently required. To start computation before the purpose of the problem is clear and before the conditions are well in mind is a most inefficient habit. Out of discussions about the relationship of reading to success in mathematics should come the idea that cumulative technical vocabulary, formulas, signs and symbols are specialized forms of reading. Reading problems call for extreme concentration, selective thinking, and clearly logical reasoning on the part of the students. Reading in no other subject is quite so demanding. It is an advanced form of thinking, often quite abstract.

Mathematical materials require that students think in an orderly and logical way as they read. They must see clearly that conditions 1 and 2 must necessarily lead to condition 3; that angles and arcs are, or are not, equivalent; that the conditions in one problem are actually quite different from those in another that is stated somewhat similarly. In addition, the students must think selectively as they try to identify the data and details essential to the solution and must disregard any that can and should be ignored. Selective thinking is also necessary as they decide on exactly what they are to find as an answer to the problem.

The importance of vocabulary. Another distinguishing feature of mathematical materials is the technicality of the vocabulary. There are many specialized terms, such as *cone, sine, angle of depression, tangent, coefficient, radical, reciprocal, perpendicular, acute angle,* and *diagonal.* In the more advanced phases of mathematics, authors of textbooks tend to write as though the vocabulary of the simpler phases of the subject has been completely mastered before going on to the higher levels. The cumulative vocabulary of mathematics can be a major hurdle in students' reading of textbooks if the teacher has failed to clinch required technical vocabulary as successive courses have been taught. The teacher should plan specific ways of developing specialized vocabulary. One way might be to write the new term on the chalkboard as he pronounces it and help the students find it in the text. They should be encouraged to define it because of relationship to other words, context clues, or supporting material that hints at its meaning. For example, *concentric* appears in a study of circles. To the question, "Is there any part of this word that reminds you of some other word?" should come two ideas. One that the prefix *con* means *with* and *centric* resembles *center, central,* and perhaps *centrifugal.* What, then, might concentric circles be? *With, center*–circles with the same center could be developed and then checked with the glossary for confirmation. In geometry, *polygon, pentagon, hexagon,* and *octagon* contain common elements; they also contain prefixes that probably have been met in other words–*polysyllabic* and *octave,* for example. When the root *gon* is identified as corner and the prefixes as the number of corners, the words have meaning for the student and will probably be retained as permanent learning.

Some of the words that need special attention are those that take on a new and different meaning in mathematics as compared to already familiar uses. *Product, rate, base, interest, root, literal,* and *regular* have different connotations in mathematics. Recalling customary meanings may becloud the mathematics setting. Since the words seem deceptively easy, many teachers never pause to make sure that the mathematical connotation is being used.

An integral part of mathematics courses is the reading and interpretation of problems. In the verbal problem students must learn the importance of methodical, precise reading. They must come to realize that almost every word is crucial to complete understanding of the problem. Recognizing all the words, applying their mathematical meanings, and sensing the respective relationship among the several conditions are prerequisites to choice of computation process.

One technique to sharpen students' critical thinking in mathematical reading is to assign problems in which data are incomplete. Thoughtful reading should quickly detect the omission. In a similar way, extraneous and irrelevant facts should be spotted immediately.

If some of the students have unusual difficulty in solving problems, the teacher might ask them to read several problems orally. Doing this will indicate to a degree the type of reading difficulty they are experiencing—faulty word recognition, failure to grasp thought units, or lack of mathematical concepts. Whenever students can solve problems that are read to them but cannot read independently they show evidence of reading retardation and should be considered for remedial placement.

Handling assignments efficiently. Systematic attack on mathematics assignments should be learned from the beginning of a course. A characteristic of mathematics is its orderliness and this applies equally to learning its content. Basic concepts and specialized vocabulary must be mastered for success in this field. Time spent in helping students follow definite procedures of careful reading, putting the facts to use, and evaluating the solution by rereading the problem will prove its value to the student who embarks upon secondary mathematics. To say this another way—in the early training of mathematics students, *reading* is probably of equal value to *computation.*

Teachers of mathematics probably more easily accept responsibility for teaching reading in connection with their subject than do teachers of other content fields. Reading, like mathematics, has been taught throughout the elementary school but many students have lacked the maturity to operate effectively with either reading or mathematical skills before the secondary school age. Teachers of science, homemaking, industrial arts, and business education often find it necessary to reteach both basic reading and mathematical skills.

While more students in *general mathematics* and *beginning algebra* will need direction about mathematical reading, there will be those in advanced courses such as trigonometry who could profit from reading suggestions. The modern textbook of advanced mathematics contains considerable reading material on the analytical aspects of the subject and a reduced number of problems to solve in comparison to textbooks of a decade ago. The student at this level must be able to read with thorough understanding in order to apply the proper procedures to the variety of problems included in an exercise.

Problem analysis. Almost all textbooks contain the steps in attacking word problems. The importance of this systematic approach to mathematical computation should be impressed upon the students. The steps are variously stated but in essence the following is inclusive:

1. *Work on one problem at a time.*
2. Read the problem carefully.
3. Reread it and determine what it is about (main idea).
4. What are the conditions (details)?
5. What are you asked to find?
6. What is the order in which the conditions of the problem should be used?
7. What processes are required?
8. What is a reasonable answer?
9. Perform the necessary operations, compare with your estimate, go back to the reading of the problem if the answer seems unreasonable.

If students grasp the fact that any well-worded problem consists of a main idea (purpose) and details (conditions governing the problem situation) they will more readily see that reading is a fundamental part of the mathematics program. They will understand that by following each step, keeping in mind its relationship to the other steps, the processes for solving the problem can be more readily determined. Unless students can read carefully enough to see the relationship of the facts to each other and to the main idea they are incapable of achieving much success. A supplementary technique in assisting students to determine the main idea and important details in a problem is to ask them to indicate key words or phrases, word cues to solution (*what is the total, how much more is needed, how many times*), and the question that is the basic part of the problem.

Following directions. Ability to follow directions is a feature of mathematics, especially in the area of geometry. How to construct figures, how to circumscribe, how to bisect, and how to measure are familiar assignments. Only accurate reading will produce the desired result.

Formulas in arithmetic and algebra. Formulas become useful as abbreviations in arithmetic. Pupils learn that the area of a triangle is ½ ab or that the area of a rectangle is $A = lw$. These formulas have been usable features of arithmetic as the learner has substituted numbers for the letters and has worked specific problems. When the student embarks upon algebra he is to learn that letters are convenient to express relationships among quantities. $8x - 4y = 8z$, where x is 4, y is 2, and z is 3, is an algebraic equation. Algebraic equations are extremely convenient in solving problems. The only difference between arithmetic and algebra is the degree to which letters represent numbers. Accurate reading is required if algebraic equations are to be stated correctly.

Another feature of algebra is the groupings through use of brackets and parentheses. If students have been taught to read $11 - 6 = 5$ as a sentence, then the algebraic arrangement of groups will not be difficult. In modern mathematics emphasis is being placed upon the grouping of quantities as a sentence that requires punctuation for clarification. The statement $16 - 4 \times 7$ is an ambiguous statement. If the reader punctuates it to read $16 - (4 \times 7)$, the answer is -12.

However, if the statement is read $(16-4) \times 7$, the answer is 84. In algebra much of the work will require simplifying expressions in which signs of aggregation as well as positive and negative signs preceding the enclosing marks will be important.

Positive and negative numbers also require thoughtful reading. The tendency to think of these signs as indicators of processes must be superseded by the idea that this type of number indicates magnitudes that are thought of as opposite in direction ($26°$ compared with $-6°$).

The modern world is finding growing need for communicating much of the world's knowledge through mathematical expressions. For functional literacy of the citizens of a democracy the field of mathematics becomes increasingly important. Competency in reading and interpreting quantitative language and data is a reasonable expectancy of secondary education.

Summary

Reading in mathematics demands care and thought. In contrast to much of the material the student reads in the secondary school, mathematical material is concise. Mathematics demands highly critical reading—full understanding of all types of reading accompanied by thinking.

The cumulative effect of vocabulary, formulas, principles, and notation is probably greater than in any other subject.

Today's world is making greater use of the language of mathematics as a tool of effective communication; secondary students should, therefore, become efficient readers and interpreters of quantitative discourse.

Suggested Readings

EAGLE, EDWIN. "The Relationship of Certain Reading Abilities to Success in Mathematics," *Mathematics Teacher,* XLI (April, 1948), 175–79.

FEHR, HOWARD F. "General Ways to Identify Students with Scientific and Mathematical Potential," *Mathematics Teacher,* XLVI (April, 1953), 230–34.

Five Steps to Reading Success in Science, Social Studies, and Mathematics. New York: Metropolitan School Study Council, 1954.

FLEMING, ROBERT E. "Mathematics and Its English," *School Science and Mathematics,* LIII (October, 1953), 601–2.

LEARY, BERNICE E. "Improving Reading Skills in Mathematics and Science," *High School Journal,* XXXVI (October, 1952), 17–21.

Teaching Reading in the High School. Kansas Studies in Education, Vol. 10. Lawrence, Kan.: University of Kansas Publications, February, 1960. Pp. 23–29.

The Suggestion Box

If the textbook does not contain study helps in reading, ask the students to describe how they approached the mathematics assignment. Have the logs read and select from the descriptions the portions that would make a good sequence of steps. Be sure to include the major difficulties encountered by the students.

Ask students to read newspapers and magazines to locate any references to the topic under discussion in the classroom. As a class exercise build a set of problems from the data.

Have students study the vocabulary for any particular section of the text. Ask them to listen for, or find in print, any of the terms they have been studying. Have them describe the specific situation in which the term occurred.

Collect as many types of graphs as can be found in one week in newspapers and magazines. Have individuals in the class interpret them. Ask the students to prepare a bulletin board display of graphs of all types to inform the students and faculty of activities of the school. Be sure they read carefully to decide the type of graph most adaptable to certain kinds of data.

Have students read books on the history of mathematics or the biographies of great mathematicians. What information did they find that would assist them to build greater appreciation and understanding of the subject?

XII

Reading in Industrial Arts

THE TECHNICAL CHARACTER OF READING REQUIRED
in much of the industrial arts can be illustrated by an article,
"Workshop on the Wall," which appeared in the July, 1955,
issue of *Popular Science*. The article describes how a folding
workshop can be constructed along the wall of a garage for
storing tools at all times, with ample space for parking a car.
The text is accompanied by illustrative photographs and a
blueprint layout with directions for building the shelves and
installing the equipment. The article starts:

Here is one workshop layout that won't elbow your car out of
the garage or start a feud with your wife over basement laundry
space. It's built around three ingenious workshop pieces:

A workbench that folds up as the door of a roomy tool cabinet.

A rolling accessory chest, doubling as an outboard support for
long work.

Wall-hugging shelves that hold heavy attachments where you
can get them with the least effort.

These were designed by the Magna Engineering Corporation
especially for use with Shopsmith equipment. Because of its shape

and caster mounting, this combination tool can be stored under the shelves.

Folding Workbench. A hardwood top almost 5′ long folds up into a wall cabinet. Inside this, there is a space 5″ deep for tools. When down, the top rests on two sturdy legs, locked by a single brace. The perforated panel, on which tools are held by pre-shaped hooks sold for the purpose, is set into grooves. Fasten the cabinet to the wall studs with its lower edges 29″ above the floor. Cut the plywood underlay for the top to size; then glue and blind nail the oak flooring over it, and oak trim to the edges. Attach the top to the cabinet floor with three 3½″ butt hinges.

Hinge the legs to the underside of the top. Notch the bottom edge of the horizontal rail for the bolt, and screw a triangular hardwood block to the brace to provide a flat surface for the wing nut. Cut a hasp across the end of its slot to form a forked end. Drill a hole in this leaf; then bolt it to the cabinet top. Bend the forked end up to match the end bevel on the brace when it's swung up.

The illustration for the folding workbench is not reproduced here. As a reader, how well do you believe you read the directions given in this article? Can you visualize the workbench and perhaps make a drawing of it? How well did you grasp the sequence of the directions? In addition to the directions quoted here, the article listed technical terms that must be understood to read the blueprint layout:

layout	washer	jig saw
rasp	wingnut	retractable casters
stopblock	bracket	chest base
rabbet	leg mounting	oak trim
brace	composition board	auger bits
stud	deep end	punches
strap hinge	circular saw	drills
lag screws	drawer slide	panel set
butt hinge	groove	lathe accessories

plywood	dowel	outboard support
flooring	sander support	base plywood
carriage bolt	jointer	cleat
slot	band saw	perforated
rail	belt sander	

Many magazines encourage the householder to make use of his leisure time by constructing furniture on a do-it-yourself basis. The woodworking and outdoor building projects described in *Sunset* magazine for any year run into hundreds of articles each for woodworking and for outdoor building such as entries, fences and screens, greenhouses, and plant shelters. Whether the adult reader can follow the detailed instructions in these articles will depend upon his reading ability in terms of handling specialized vocabulary and detailed directions.

Presumably the skills developed in the secondary school industrial arts program will be retained throughout the lifetime of many of the students. Certainly the skill of following directions for constructing articles for the home will be demanded again and again in postschool days. Whether the adult will retain the skills learned in the industrial arts program will depend, to a great degree, upon the thoroughness of the instruction given in that program; and reading for the clarification and assimilation of ideas is obviously an integral part of a successful industrial arts program.

Technical vocabulary. Consideration of the vocabulary listed in the article on the construction of a workbench is somewhat sobering to the individual when he realizes that not only must he be able to pronounce the word but he must also have a knowledge of the relationship of the word to a task, a material, or a combination of operations. The reader of the specification sheet for the construction of any article must recognize words in relation to materials or operations, follow a sequence of tasks, and visualize the actual building of the article as he reads. It is possible for a student to learn to construct simple articles in the industrial arts shop by simply following the oral directions of another person or observing the work of another student; but the final test of his proficiency as a student of the industrial arts is his ability to read and execute directions independently. Basic to his understanding of the processes involved is a knowledge of the vocabulary used. The *Denver Instructional Guide in Industrial Arts*, 1952, gives the following vocabulary lists for metalwork in the secondary school:

1st and 2nd Semesters—Junior High

Words describing materials, equipment, or operations, or words having special meanings.

acid	flux	planish
aluminum	forge	raise
anneal	form	rule
anvil	foundry	rust
blast	galvanized	sand
bolt	goggles	sheet
brake	harden	smelt
brass	hem	snips
bronze	ingot	solder
caps	iron	steel
casting	lead	sweat
chip	melt	tang
cone	metal	temper
copper	mold	tongs
flask	nut	vent
folder	ore	wrench

Supplementary words:

angle	bristle	metallic
bright	level	smooth

1st Semester—Senior High

Words describing materials, equipment, or operations, or words having special meanings:

acetylene	flange	riddle
alloy	follow-block	riser
ampere	fulcrum	rouge
arc	fusion	sal ammoniac
asbestos	gate	scale
beakhorn	guard	scraper
beeswax	handwheel	seam
blowhole	helmet	shaper
blowhorn	hone	shear
carriage	hydrochloric	silver
caseharden	knurl	slick
centerdrill	lacquer	sprue
clearance	micrometer	swab
compound	monel	swing
cope	muriatic	tallow
cupola	nickel	taper
crucible	oxyacetylene	torch
disc	oxygen	trowel
draft	pewter	twist
drag	rake	tungsten
envelope	radius	volt
faceplate	rammer	weld
fillet	rap	wiring

Supplementary words:

apprentice	corrode	grease
automatic	diagonal	hexagon
blacksmith	diameter	machinist

Supplementary words:

| circumference | equipment | pressure |
| compute | elastic | tinsmith |

Several approaches to the teaching of technical vocabulary for the industrial arts can be effective:

1. Direct teaching of the word as it appears in the daily lesson, illustrating it with the material, the tool, or the operation.
2. Providing pictures or drawings of the essential materials or tools in the student's handbook.
3. Labeling, in their appropriate positions on tool racks or in materials' storage cabinets, the various articles used or referred to in a simple task.
4. Using the dictionary to learn the correct pronunciation and perhaps the interesting histories of the words.
5. Constructing a dictionary of industrial arts terms. (To do this glue the alphabetized entries on large sheets—approximately $2' \times 3'$—of masonite or plywood and attach the "pages" to a rack which is accessible to the students in the shop. Illustrations for each entry would be helpful.)

Reading in industrial arts. The *Course of Study in General Metal* in the Sacramento City Unified School District, 1948, presents for the beginning eighth grade an exploratory course in sheet metal. The following safety precautions represent a type of difficult reading characteristic of industrial arts:

1. Select the correct tools and machines.
2. Make certain that the equipment is in good working condition.
3. Follow the correct procedures in any operation.
4. Use caution while handling sheet metal.
5. Don't let sheet of metal slip through the hands.
6. Always pick up a soldering copper by the handle.
7. Do not have hands or any part of the body in front of a soldering furnace when it is being ignited.

8. Always carry sharp-pointed tools and metal with the pointed or sharp edges facing downward.
9. Be sure you understand your job. You learn by asking questions. The dangerous, awkward worker is the one who fears to ask questions.
10. Know all the dangers and hazards of the tools and machines used in sheet-metal work and use the necessary precautions.

Why are these statements so difficult to read? Because their full significance is not known until the student has become familiar with working with sheet metal. Knowing through doing is necessary for true understanding, appreciation, and acquisition of skills. There must be precision in reading as well as in measuring, in cutting, and in making joints.

Reading in the industrial arts combines understanding the meanings of technical terms, perceiving the relationship between different parts of the sentence and different sentences and paragraphs, relating what is already known through experience to the new step to be learned, and following the directions exactly in the sequence suggested. The test of correct reading is the demonstrated ability to do what the description calls for. Contrasted to easy fast reading of a simple narrative, following directions calls for deliberate reading and exact application of ideas expressed in words, phrases, or short sentences and often rereading to check on the required sequence in action.

The following methods of presentation are required in the teaching in the industrial arts:

1. Demonstrations
2. Oral questioning and discussion

3. Motion pictures and filmstrips
4. Instruction sheets
5. Tests
6. Reference books, drawings, blueprints.

While the methods of presentation are being developed, the directions for doing are being observed. The student cannot retain nor recall all that has been seen or done except by rereading the directions. It is fortunate that printed material is available for rereading so that all that has been presented can be re-created. Only reading material has the quality of permanence.

Industrial arts library. In order to satisfy the existing need for strengthening and expanding the instructions given by the teacher to his students, the industrial arts shop library is essential. Detailed information concerning the fundamental operations on the projects cannot be satisfactorily taught unless some printed material is easily accessible.

The reasons for the industrial arts library are many. It aids the interested student in:

1. Developing an appreciation for the advances in modern industrial products, for workmanship and design, along with developing his skill in the fundamental processes of interpreting drawings and illustrations.
2. Choosing a vocation in which he may determine his capabilities, limitations, and interests.
3. Planning and problem solving.
4. Making use of leisure time, both as a hobby and as the "handy man" about the home, through the use of detailed information.

Because one book cannot adequately cover all subjects equally well, there is a definite need for a variety of books:

1. project or problem books   4. magazines
2. shop manuals   5. occupational books
3. reference books

The project or problem book, in most cases, furnishes new and varied ideas, drawings and designs that may be used in the shop. In order to use this book the student must already possess a certain basic knowledge of the use of tools. The shop manual serves the purpose of furnishing working directions and other data, such as lists of requisite materials, drawings, and tools to be used. Reference books give information concerning the special use of tools, equipment, or materials and for comparing methods of solving problems. Magazines are of inestimable value to the shop library in conveying current information to the students and teachers. Occupation books present information concerning the various occupations at which men work and assist the students in their selection of an occupation. While these books generally are to be found in the vocational guidance library, perhaps they would be more widely used if they were on hand in the industrial arts shop area. A clean place to read is a must!

Summary

Reading in the industrial arts is generally not a simple process, despite the fact that directions appear to be terse and well organized. In addition, many students who register for industrial arts courses are not successful in the "academic" courses and are seeking an area in which they can succeed. Often these students are further frustrated when they learn that the industrial arts program demands reading skill for which they have had no preparation. It becomes the responsibility of the industrial arts teacher, then, to teach the skills of reading required for successful achievement in the shop. These skills include the understanding and knowledge of technical terms; reading and following directions, both in details and in sequence; and reading for further understanding of materials, equipment, and operations.

Suggested Readings

STRUCK, F. T. "102 Key Words," *Industrial Arts and Vocational Education,* XXXII (February, 1943), 57.

SUERKEN, E. H. "Basic Glossary and Vocabulary in Printing," *Industrial Arts and Vocational Education,* XLI (November, 1952), 305–7.

"Reading Skills and Habits Needed in the Industrial Arts," *Teaching Reading in the High School.* Lawrence, Kan.: University of Kansas Publications, February, 1960. Pp. 30–32.

WILLIAMS, S. L., and ANDERSON, S. A. "Power of Words in Industrial Arts," *American Vocational Journal,* XXVII (December, 1953), 12.

The Suggestion Box

Several tool and equipment firms distribute filmstrips and sound films on the use of their products; these may be used to motivate the industrial arts class to read.

Using pictures in magazines, catalogues, or trade journals, have the students draw working plans for various objects; "reading" an illustration thus becomes important.

Consult magazines and newspapers for advertisements of tools, materials, and products which relate to the industrial arts program. Compare specifications and prices. This provides an opportunity to study the propaganda of advertising.

Encourage students to read pamphlets and articles which give information on vocational possibilities in the industrial arts. The head of the counseling program can give assistance in locating these materials.

After the students have read the specifications for a simple task in the shop, ask them to close their manuals, and write down, step by step, the processes and materials involved.

XIII

Reading in Other Subject Areas

CERTAIN SUBJECT AREAS OF THE SECONDARY
school have unique phases which must be considered if the
high school reading program is to be complete. Much of
what has been said in the preceding chapters can be adapted
for use in any subject area of the curriculum. The instructor
should be guided in the choice of reading skills to fit the
objectives of a particular subject, the amount and type of
reading materials used, and adult needs for information in
that subject area. Consideration is given in this chapter to
reading in music and homemaking; other subject areas such
as physical education, business education, and art make
similar demands on the student for reading carefully and
selectively. The teacher of any of these areas will find suggestions for helping students to improve their reading abilities in the preceding chapters and in this one.

Music

The teacher of music should regard as reasonable the
statement that the student of music has need for good read-

ing skills and that a responsibility of the teacher is to aid students in developing those reading skills which are pertinent to the study of music in its many phases. For instance, the technical vocabulary of music requires careful study and the development of skills of rapid recognition. A study of vocal music certainly demands that the student be able to recognize and understand words quickly and efficiently and to develop a sense of proper phrasing, which is dictated by both the music and the lyrics. Reading for understanding of the lives and times of composers, the development of forms of music, the fascinating evolution of musical instruments, and the stories of great operas and other musical forms demands skills which are both general to all reading and occasionally specific to the reading of the literature of music. The music teacher should be sensitive to the reading needs of his students and be prepared to give guidance in the development of specific skills.

Little is known of the correlation between general reading ability and the reading of a musical score; we have sufficient evidence, however, to point out that many students who read musical scores and perform brilliantly in both instrumental and vocal music do not read well when confronted with the printed page. Conversely, many students who have highly developed skills for reading widely are unable to transfer those skills to the reading of musical scores, even with considerable training. Certainly perception plays a role in both types of reading, and the student who has developed skills of keen perception in all general academic areas is usually capable of reading music well.

Scanning is one skill which the student of music must

develop, and all good musicians have developed this skill.
For instance, when the student examines a piece of music
for the first time he scans immediately for key, orchestration
or arrangement, shifts in key or time, phrasing, and many
other pertinent factors. This initial scanning is usually followed by a more careful perusal of the score, "reading" a
part or parts; in the case of a vocal selection, the student
may read the lyrics and attempt to fit them to the music.
The teacher of music should give careful direction to the
student for the development of skill in this type of scanning
and subsequent familiarization with the score.

Vocabulary peculiar to the study of music is often difficult
and unfamiliar to the student who is beginning his study of
music. The terms that describe the various musical forms,
such as *fugue, opera, concerto,* and *motet,* should be taught
both by careful examination of scores and by providing
opportunities for listening to representative examples. Terms
used to create both color and mood, such as *andante, piu
animato, molto meno mosso, sempre,* and *allegro,* are often
very difficult for the beginner. They require a careful examination by the reader, translation from the Italian to English
to make them more understandable, and examples through
the use of instruments or voice. An important form of comprehension occurs at the moment of instant recognition and
appropriate reaction to these musical terms.

Reading for information about the history and development of music is a skill which the student of music should
be encouraged to develop. Many students who are not
capable of performing on an instrument or with the voice
may develop deep appreciation of music. The more these

students can learn about the composers, the stories behind the compositions, and the intricacies of musical forms the better chance they have for deepening their appreciation of good music. Reading of biographies of composers and musicians, the involved stories of many of the great operas, and technical discussions of musical forms and their development require skills of locating information, reading for main ideas and details, organizing information, and reacting to what is read. Guidelines for the development of these skills have been outlined in Chapter VI.

Students who do not read well can still share in the wealth of information that is available in the literature of music. Lives of composers, stories of the great operas, and histories of the instruments have been written in simple language for the less capable reader. The teacher of music should consult the librarian for lists of books available for the student of the history and appreciation of music. The librarian can aid the teacher in determining the reading level of each book. On the basis of the book list and the difficulty levels, the teacher is then in a good position to recommend materials for the individual reader.

Reading and discussing musical criticism is an excellent means of aiding the student to develop skills of critical reading and thinking. Available in practically any newspaper of a metropolitan center is the column of the music critic. Realizing that students and adults alike are prone to accept as fact that which appears in print, perhaps the teacher of music could suggest some criteria for judging the validity of criticism, such as:

1. What is the reputation of the particular critic? Is he a recognized authority on music of all types?

2. Does the critic reveal, through the language he uses, his depth of the knowledge of the subject?
3. Does the critic reveal his personal prejudices and biases? For instance, does this critic consistently berate jazz and laud the symphony, no matter how poor the performance of the latter might have been or how superior the performance of the former?
4. Was the criticism general, or was it directed at minor technical details?
5. If you attended the performance, how does your reaction compare to the reactions stated by the critic? Has reading his criticism caused you to alter your opinions?
6. How does this particular critic's appraisal of a performance compare or contrast to the appraisal given by another critic?

Other criteria, of course, might be added. Important to the student is the development of awareness of the fact that a critic is just another person expressing his personal opinions and that those opinions may or may not represent critical judgment.

The music teacher regards the development of interests, tastes, and appreciations in music as a vital factor in the teaching of music to the student. In a complex society, whose members are often harassed, often overworked, frequently besieged by worries and frustrations, and constantly in search of satisfying leisure-time activities, the teacher believes that the understanding and appreciation of the world's fabulous wealth of good music may offer solace, entertainment, and deep pleasure to the individual. To develop students who one day will become adults who will regard good music as an indispensable part of living, the teacher must work not only toward the development of technical skills of performance but also toward the improvement of the skills of listening, observing, and reading.

Homemaking

Homemaking has become an important instructional area of the secondary school. The course offerings in this field cover a wide range: clothing, foods, diet and nutrition, infant and child care, home nursing, personal grooming, home planning, and budgeting.

Since many students who are programmed into home-making courses are often not outstanding academically, efficient reading is often a problem to students and teachers alike. Much of the content of homemaking must be learned through the printed word. What steps should the home-making instructor take to aid students to profit from reading assignments? The reading problems in this subject area fall into two main divisions: (1) the wide variety of reading materials necessary for covering the broad range of home-making subjects and (2) the special vocabulary necessary for full understanding of those subjects.

Kinds of reading. Narration comprises one large part of the textbook material in homemaking subjects. Description and informational material may not be particularly difficult for those students who have fairly adequate general reading ability; for those less competent, introductory work before the actual reading of a textbook may be necessary. This introductory activity would include a general overview of the subject matter, specific attention to key words, and a few general questions to guide selection of pertinent ideas. Students should be told that this kind of material in the textbook can be read with greater speed and with less re-reading than other sections of the book. Full explanation of the relationship of illustrations, topical headings, italicized or underlined sections, and framed or boxed information should be given to the students. If the first one or two chapters are studied by the class as a whole under careful teacher guidance, efficient use of the book may be enhanced.

The elliptical language of recipes, patterns, and directions requires particularly careful reading, since the reader is expected to depend heavily on previous knowledge:

Drop raw prawns into boiling salted water and cook until tender. Drain, peel, and cut out the black vein down the back. Set aside.

The reader might reasonably question: How much salt? How does one judge tenderness of a prawn? What implement should be used to cut out the vein?

Reading to follow directions. Any branch of homemaking makes heavy demands on the student to read and follow directions. This kind of reading is slow, painstaking, and thorough. While other subject-matter teachers will be concerned with the development of this skill also, the homemaking instructors have a particular responsibility for guiding students in the acquisition of a skill that will be of major importance throughout life. Most of the students will become homemakers. Day after day they will be called upon to prepare meals; to buy wisely; to use and care for appliances; and to make home a comfortable, safe, and happy place.

The first step in reading directions is to skim over the material to get a general idea of what is involved in each particular case. This rapid overview should prepare the reader for a sequence of activities: preheating an oven, chilling or heating ingredients, selecting utensils, and allowing a block of time to finish the job under way. A slower, more thorough reading will then be necessary. Directions require the reader to think in terms of steps and to follow those steps exactly. A rereading is usually necessary to determine if all the instructions have been carried out. Constant practice of this way of reading directions will enable students to carry out directions with a minimum of waste of materials and unsuccessful experiences.

Part of the reading of directions will include understanding of arithmetical expressions, charts, graphs, diagrams, and individual items. Each of these demands a slightly different reading from purely narrative material. A check should be occasionally made to determine how much instruction is necessary to make these phases of reading meaningful to the students. Silent reading followed by oral reading, discussion, and demonstration will help to establish accuracy. For example, if a recipe states that the thermostat on the stove should be set at 375° and that the required baking time is 45 minutes, these facts should be read and then actually followed by setting the thermostat and the timer.

Another need in this type of reading is concerned with instructions about the use and care of appliances and household products. Not only is this a matter of dollars and cents, but human life also may be involved. Electrical and gas appliances do much of the work of the home today; they must be used with full awareness of their potential danger if not handled correctly and carefully. Many household products also need utmost care in their use and storage. Highly flammable products must be used with caution; poisonous substances must be stored out of reach of children and away from possible contact with food. Manufacturers supply directions and instructions with all these products; careful reading should guarantee that the consumer is at least informed of the specific directions for handling a product.

The homemaking teacher may help her students to become more skilled at following printed directions if she promotes activities during the class period which involve rapid reading for:

1. Discovering, generally, the task to be performed
2. Determining the ingredients, materials, or utensils needed
3. Noting the steps to be followed and their exact sequence
4. Noting any precautions which are stated.

Critical reading. Not only does the student in homemaking courses need to do careful reading, but she must do critical reading. From the myriad of products advertised and displayed, the modern homemaker must be able to select those that adequately meet the needs of her family. Labels on canned and frozen foods, tags on garments and yardage, descriptions of household appliances, and sales information require evaluative reading. The product with the lowest price may not always be the most economical when all factors have been weighed and considered. Extravagant claims made by manufacturers need common-sense analysis to decide if they are true. The finest print may contain the most significant information. Students should be given ample practice in reading advertisements, labels, and brochures to develop this reading skill. Investigation, experimentation, and discussion should follow to substantiate or disqualify claims.

Vocabulary. As in other content areas, both general and specialized vocabulary in homemaking subjects must be learned and interpreted. Care should be taken with words that may be readily recognized but whose precise meaning in context may not be clear. For instance, the following direction is often given in a cake or cooky recipe:

Cream the butter and sugar.

The experienced cook realizes that she is not required to add cream to the two ingredients mentioned! This, however, is an example of many terms used in homemaking tasks which may have meanings in other contexts. *Fold* as applied in cooking will be less adequately understood than when used in a discussion of clothing; *bias* may be remembered from a social studies text but requires a different meaning when it is met in sewing. The list of words of general vocabulary that take on specialized meaning in homemaking is lengthy, and when words of multiple meanings occur homemaking teachers should take time to make certain that meanings are clarified and related to the particular task being studied. Vocabulary charts (illustrated when possible) may be used frequently to clarify meanings of complex tasks.

For many students the review of word-attack skills may be necessary. Hearing words, seeing them, and using them will contribute to mastery. Picture and context clues should be emphasized. Glossaries should be studied; and the key to pronunciation should be taught, illustrated, and frequently reviewed to give students independence in word recognition.

Summary

It is highly possible that the homemaking teacher and the musician might argue that they have no responsibility for aiding students in the improvement of reading skills; perhaps the strongest argument which can be offered in favor of these teachers being mentors of reading and study skills is that often in the secondary school students who cannot compete adequately in the areas of English, social science, and science because of their inadequate reading skills will turn to music, homemaking, or industrial arts for satisfaction of the most common personal urge—to be successful at something and to gain recognition. Certainly there is no content area which does not require careful, efficient reading; and each teacher of a content area has a dual responsibility for teaching both subject matter and the skills for mastering that subject matter.

Suggested Readings

BUDISH, B. E. "Business Education Instructor Also Teaches Reading," *Journal of Business Education,* XXX (November, 1954), 68–70.

HARRIS, THEODORE L. "Making Reading an Effective Instrument of Learning in the Content Fields," *Reading in the High School and College.* 47th Yearbook, National Society for the Study of Education. Chicago: University of Chicago Press, 1948. Pp. 116–33.

HOUSE, FOREST W. "Are You Solving the Reading Problem in Bookkeeping?" *Business Educational World,* XXXIII (February, 1953), 291–92.

MEHRER, RON. "Improving Reading Ability of Vocational Agriculture Students," *Agricultural Education Magazine,* XXXII (October, 1959), 81–82.

MUSSELMAN, VERNON A. "The Reading Problem in Teaching Bookkeeping," *Business Education Forum,* XIV (December, 1959), 5–7.

NYE, R. E. "If You Don't Use Syllables, What Do You Use?" *Music Educator's Journal,* XXXIX (April, 1953), 41–42.

SPACHE, GEORGE D. "Types and Purposes of Reading in Various Curriculum Fields," *The Reading Teacher*, XI (February, 1958), 158–64.

The Suggestion Box

Encourage students to keep a notebook of words which are specific to the vocabulary of a content area, writing each one in context which will explain its meaning.

Make a search of words which have different meanings in different areas. A good example is the word *baste*, which means one thing in cooking but another in sewing; the word has still another meaning, not associated with either of the above uses.

Compare the criticisms of an opera or recital, as written by two different critics in different newspapers.

In the homemaking and business education classes, compare advertisements which appear in different periodicals for the same type of product. What propaganda devices are used by advertisers in selling their product to the reader? How does the illustration affect the reader's reactions to the product?

XIV

The Remedial Program

PLANNING A REMEDIAL READING PROGRAM FOR THE
secondary school requires several special considerations
which are not normally associated with the developmental
reading program. Whereas in the classroom the subject-
matter teacher can, with training in developmental skills,
teach the reading skills pertinent to the maturity level of the
students and the difficulty of the content, the teacher of
remedial students must be trained to give instruction in the
particular therapeutic techniques which severely retarded
readers demand. Special teachers, materials, space, time,
and the students themselves are factors which must be considered in setting up the remedial program.

The teacher. Numerous teachers of remedial reading are
trained each year in teacher-training colleges or in special
reading laboratory centers. The greatest number of these
highly skilled specialists are placed in positions in elementary
schools, where it is generally possible to give assistance to
the child before his difficulties become too severe. Unfor-

tunately, there are innumerable students who do not receive this special training during their elementary school years, and they become the problems of the secondary schools. Today, increased attention is being given to the training of teachers for special reading classes in the secondary school, but the demand for such specialists far exceeds the supply. In the face of predictions of imminent teacher shortages in all areas of the curriculum, it appears that it would be wise to encourage regular subject-matter teachers to take training in the diagnosis and remediation of reading difficulties, in order that some of the problems of reading may be solved in the classroom. But, even if all teachers were skilled in techniques of teaching reading in their particular subject areas, a need would still exist for the specialist who works with those students who cannot benefit from regular instruction in the classroom. These students must be taken out of the classroom and given remedial training which is directed at their particular and peculiar needs. The processes of diagnosing needs and giving training to the severely retarded reader require a skillful teacher.

What particular skills must this teacher of remedial reading possess? Experience has pointed to the desirability of previous experience in the teaching of developmental reading to elementary school children. Many of the students in the remedial program in the secondary school are reading at levels commensurate with the skills of the children in the intermediate grades, and the most severely retarded students may not possess skills above the primary level. At whatever level the skills are found to exist, they can be more easily detected and treated by the teacher who has had experience in teaching skills at those levels.

The remedial teacher should be trained in diagnosing, both informally and formally, all types of reading difficulties. He must have a thorough knowledge of the administration and interpretation of tests of reading and related language arts, including both achievement and diagnostic types. A sound background in psychology is desirable, particularly in terms of personality disorders which may be associated with, or the cause of, reading disabilities. Since he will have close contact with his students, often in individual or small-group situations, he will be able to give aid to those students if he has experience in counseling.

It has often been observed that we have too many professionals in the field who can tell us what the difficulty is but few who can tell us what to do about it. Hence the training of the remedial teacher must include all areas of developmental reading, plus those techniques which are applied to the severely retarded reader. He must have a thorough knowledge of the materials available for correcting each type of reading difficulty; he should know how to adapt materials for particular needs.

Students who are referred to the remedial program in the secondary school come with all types of attitudes. Many are sincerely anxious to improve their skills; others, equally concerned about their difficulties, have failed successively through the elementary grades and have adopted attitudes of hostility toward reading and teachers. Still others are not yet ready to assume responsibility for improving their own skills; they are seeking a panacea, which they hope the teacher will give to them in small, painless doses. Some are ashamed of their disabilities in reading and writing, some are fearful of additional failures, and still others will work desperately and respond enthusiastically to the slightest success. The attitude of the teacher toward these remedial students—diverse as they may be in personality patterns and abilities and attitudes toward themselves and school—is obviously as important as his skills for teaching reading.

Perhaps it is unnecessary to mention what the remedial teacher should not be, but widespread practice prompts a word of caution. This teacher should not be the person on the staff who has been unsuccessful in classroom teaching or counseling and is "farmed out" to the remedial classes under the assumption that he may be successful in working with small groups of students. He should not be a teacher who is assigned to teaching remedial reading simply to complete a full teaching schedule. Finally, he must not be a "do-gooder." The remedial teacher should be a professionally trained teacher who assumes his responsibilities with respect for the students he will teach and with enthusiasm for the real possibilities of aiding students in improving themselves personally and scholastically.

Equally important as the teacher's relationships with his students are his relations with other faculty members and parents. The remedial student is registered in several courses besides the remedial reading class; it is vitally important that the remedial teacher communicate to other teachers, and parents, his diagnosis of the reading disability and the particular areas in which teachers and parents can help the student with his problem of reading. The severely retarded reader is usually a person who has social and emotional problems which can be relieved only by a concerted effort on the part of all people who are working with him. Through careful diagnosis, the reading teacher may determine that other teachers are making demands on the student which are far beyond his ability to produce; if this is so, the subject-matter teacher should be apprised of the student's capacity for learning, and with the careful guidance of the reading teacher a satisfactory program may be worked out for the student.

Materials. Never before in the history of publication have we had so many materials available for the teaching of remedial reading as we have today. The problem is obtaining the materials and controlling their use.

The teacher should be aware of the many bibliographies of adapted materials which are readily available for selection of suitable books and drill materials. *Fare for the Reluctant Reader, Gateways to Readable Books,* and *Good Books for Poor Readers* are among the many bibliographies which are listed in the Appendix. These sources should prove invaluable to the teacher of reading, since they provide both interest and difficulty levels of books available in most libraries.

Innumerable series of easy-to-read books are on the market, and they are being used successfully in many remedial programs. The "Deep Sea Adventures Series" (Harr-Wagner) has recently become very popular with high school students, who find in these books real satisfaction of their interests and success in reading a book independently. Other series are listed in Appendix B.

Many teachers of English object to the use of simplified classics, but these books can be used to real advantage with retarded readers. The young person who cannot read the original version of a book is cut off from participation in classroom activities and discussions. If proper controls are exercised, in terms of limiting the use of the simplified

classics to those students who cannot benefit from the regular text, these books can be used to fill a real need. They
should not be placed on the open shelves of the library; they
can be controlled only if they are placed in the special
reading room and used in the remedial classes.

Secondary school teachers often complain that many of
the workbook-type materials are not appropriate for their
students, since most of the workbooks have been written
for the elementary school child. Many of these workbooks
are extremely helpful in the remedial program if they are
properly introduced to the student. Consider the case of Ben:

A sophomore in high school, Ben, 16, was a severely retarded
reader. His achievement scores in vocabulary and comprehension
were at the primary level of 3.2 and 2.8, respectively. The reading teacher administered a Gilmore Oral Reading Test and the
McKee Phonetic Inventory to Ben and found that the boy was
virtually lacking in word-attack skills. His knowledge of phonics
and structural analysis was very weak; his sight vocabulary,
tested on the Dolch List of 220 Words, was extremely inadequate.

Ben could read materials at a second-reader level. He was
given a copy of the first book in the "Jim Forest Series," and he
read it with great satisfaction and discussed it enthusiastically
with his teacher. For the first time in his life, Ben had read a
"whole" book. The teacher talked to Ben about his lack of word-
attack, word-meaning skills and told him frankly that he was in
need of practice in phonetic and structural analysis of words.
She showed Ben a copy of *Eye and Ear Fun*, Book 3, and discussed with him the work he could do independently in the
workbook. Ben agreed that it would be a good idea to try this
particular workbook. At the end of two weeks, Ben had worked
the exercises in Book 3 and had discussed each day's progress
with his teacher. His enthusiasm mounted with each day's accomplishments. For the first time, he was gaining an understanding of how to attack new words. Along with his work in the

workbook, he was reading books which the teacher had helped him select from the shelves—all at third- and fourth-reader levels. When he had finished with *Eye and Ear Fun*, he wanted something more advanced, and he received a copy of Book 4.

At the end of the semester, Ben was reading with ease at the fifth-reader level. He had a good knowledge of word-attack skills, including syllabication, and he had read over forty books. The reading teacher had talked with all of Ben's teachers in the high school, and he had received encouragement and help from each of them; the history teacher had helped Ben find books which he could read for each assignment, and Ben was participating in class discussions.

The point of this case is obvious. The reading teacher did not at any time apologize to Ben for the level of the material she provided for him. She helped Ben face his problem honestly; consequently, Ben developed no negative attitudes toward "baby" materials. For the first time in his school life Ben had experienced success in reading, and each day had brought an increased level of competency and greater feelings of satisfaction.

If the remedial program is to be regarded as a necessary part of the secondary school curriculum, then funds must be set aside in the budget for materials—a wide variety of materials at all levels of interest and reading difficulty. The reading teacher must have a room in which the materials are available to the students; the students should be free to select books to read and they should have many opportunities to discuss their reading with their teacher and other members of the reading group.

Filmstrips, practice films, recordings, workbooks, simplified classics, and a wide variety of books on all subjects and at all levels of difficulty should be made available in the reading room. Much of the material used in the remedial reading program can be taken to the reading room on permanent loan from the school library, but most of the practice materials will have to be ordered by the reading teacher for exclusive use in the reading program.

Space. As one views the status today of remedial reading programs in many secondary schools one finds that teachers are often forced to meet their remedial groups in boiler rooms, offices, cloakrooms, and any other cubbyhole that is not ordinarily in use by other teachers. Since the remedial group is generally not greater than ten in number, administrators frequently find it difficult to justify the use of a classroom for the remedial reading program. Yet adequate space *must* be provided if the program is to be a success.

The ideal situation is one in which a classroom is designed with open shelves for materials, comfortable desks which can be moved for flexible grouping, good lighting, and a pleasing and inviting color scheme for draperies, walls, and furniture. The teacher should have a conference desk, in a corner of the room where he can work individually with students or with a small group. Filmstrip viewers (table type), a film projector and screen, a tape recorder for recording the students' oral reading, a record player (for use with such materials as the Enrichment Records), and a chalkboard should be available at all times.

The reading room should be one to which students like to come each day and one in which they feel comfortable and free to move about as their activities demand movement.

Time. If a remedial program is being initiated, it is wise to move slowly and cautiously during the first year, solving each problem as it arises. A pilot study is often initiated, in many secondary schools, with twenty or twenty-five students, demanding three or four hours of the time of a teacher each day. The time spent in the reading laboratory should ordinarily not exceed forty minutes for any student, unless he remains for independent reading. If the teacher meets his students in groups of five, he can meet several groups each day; as he works with one group on the correction of specific difficulties, another group can be working in the room on independent activities such as viewing filmstrips which demonstrate principles of word-attack, word-meaning skills; reading books which they have selected; working on assigned materials in practice manuals; working as a group on choral reading; or other activities which the teacher directs. Not more than ten students should be in a remedial group in a single period; if the students are severely retarded, the group should not exceed five in number.

Where, then, does the teacher find time for this program? It must be emphasized that no program can be carried out successfully unless the time element is carefully planned. No remedial program can survive unless the teacher is free of other duties and is assigned specifically for a block of time to the reading room.

Scheduling students for the reading period will present problems. Most students are already tightly scheduled, regardless of the size of the school. The most common practice in effect in secondary schools is that of releasing the student from a scheduled course to go to the reading class for two or three periods each week; conflicts occasionally arise between the subject-matter teacher and the remedial teacher. In defense of releasing the student from his regular classroom activities, we might consider this viewpoint: If the student is a severely retarded reader, he is benefiting little from regular classroom instruction, and he constitutes an instructional problem for the subject-matter teacher; hence, his seeking correction of his reading difficulties in the remedial reading program is advantageous to himself and to all his teachers.

The students. Many of the students assigned to the remedial program will be the victims of repeated failures, frequent admonitions from parents and teachers, periods of anxiety and frustration, and previous unsuccessful encounters with tutors or special teachers. It is important, then, that these students be introduced gently to reading, every effort being made by the teacher to ensure some success for each student each day—slight though that success may be.

The student who has frequently failed over a period of years in school is often a boy or girl who feels extremely unworthy in his associations with others of his age group. In the early history of his disability he most likely was confused and perplexed by concepts which he failed to grasp. Too often he became the object of shame and scorn in the classroom because of his failure to read well enough to participate in class activities. The feeling of being an unworthy reader is pervasive; soon this student feels that he is unworthy and inadequate in all things. He must be helped to realize that a reading disability is not a matter of unworthiness; it is, rather, a matter of inadequacy.

Students limited in intellectual capacity become candidates for remedial reading. The pace of the average classroom has been too much for them; they require much repetition, over a longer period of time, if they are to develop adequate concepts in any subject area. Crowded classrooms, teachers unprepared to handle the problems of the mentally deficient child, the pace of learning, inadequate materials suited to the maturity level of the retarded child—all these have contributed to the feelings of frustration which this student feels when he enters the secondary school and discovers that he simply cannot compete with most students in regular classrooms. In many of our modern secondary schools a special curriculum in special education is provided for the mentally deficient student; however, a greater number of schools do not yet provide such a program. This student *can* be taught to read, in a special reading program, at a minimal level of skills. If we could send these students from our secondary schools with skills of reading job application forms, applications for drivers' licenses, and simple specification sheets for shop tasks, we will have accomplished far more than we are now doing in the average high school program.

Some students will require only a short period of training of perhaps five or six weeks in order to become capable of proceeding independently on skills development; with others a year or more of training may be necessary before they begin to make any measurable progress. It is important that the student be apprised of his progress, from day to day and week to week, and that he learn to accept even the slightest progress as an indication of what he can eventually turn into real improvement. Graphs of reading speed, charts indicating words learned at sight, anecdotal records of daily accomplishments, and records of book reports can all be employed to help the student measure his progress.

Activities. With most of the students in a remedial program the teacher proceeds in a developmental sequence in his presentation of skills. Through careful diagnosis he knows the specific needs of each student; he may group students for drill on phonetic principles or word meanings; he may work with the total group on comprehension skills in finding main ideas and supporting details, or he may wish to work individually with one student while the others are involved in practicing a skill in their manuals. To provide motivation and variety in the program, he should also give students opportunities to dramatize stories and books; to view film-strips and films which present principles and practice in skills; to report individually to him on their progress in reading and to read aloud to the teacher in order that a continuous evaluation may be made of skills development; and to set up "teams" of two and three students who aid each other in learning particular skills.

The opportunities for providing stimulating activities for the remedial students are limitless, if the teacher has his own reading room, adequate materials, and regularly scheduled periods each week during which he can expect to work with the same students.

Summary

The remedial reading program can be successful if a well-trained remedial teacher is provided, if adequate materials are available, if space is provided specifically for the program, and if sufficient time is allotted to the program. Much of the success of the program will depend on the attitude of teachers, administrators, and students toward the necessity of supporting such a program for those students who other-

wise are doomed to continuous failure in the secondary
school classroom.

Suggested Readings

ANDERSON, IRVING. "The Concept of Remedial Reading," *Journal
of Exceptional Children,* XIII (January, 1947), 97–101.

BULLOCK, HARRISON. *Helping the Non-Reading Pupil in the
Secondary School.* New York: Bureau of Publications, Teachers
College, Columbia University, 1956.

Clinical Studies in Reading, I. Supplementary Educational Monographs, No. 68. Chicago: University of Chicago Press, 1949.

Clinical Studies in Reading, II. Supplementary Educational Monographs, No. 77. Chicago: University of Chicago Press, 1953.

CUSHMAN, C. LESLIE, and GREEN, ROSEMARY M. "Philadelphia
Schools Attack the Reading Program," *Nation's Schools,* LI
(May, 1953), 52–55.

GRAY, WILLIAM S. "How Can the Poor Reader in the Secondary
School Be Rescued?" *Bulletin of the National Association of
Secondary-School Principals,* XXXVI (April, 1952), 129–35.

GUSTAFSON, MYRTLE. "Practical Plan for Helping Retarded Readers in Secondary Schools," *California Journal of Secondary
Education,* XXX (April, 1955), 196–99.

MOHEL, ROSE. "The Remedial Reading Program at J. H. S. 240,"
High Points, XXXV (October, 1953), 25–30.

*Reading, Grades 7, 8, 9: A Teacher's Guide to Curriculum Plan-
ning.* Curriculum Bulletin No. 11, 1957–58 Series. New York:
Board of Education of the City of New York, 1959.

ROBINSON, HELEN M. *Why Pupils Fail in Reading.* Chicago: University of Chicago Press, 1946.

STRANG, RUTH. "Providing Special Help to Retarded Readers,"
Reading in the High School and College. 47th Yearbook, National Society for the Study of Education. Chicago: University
of Chicago Press, 1948. Pp. 224–50.

Teaching Reading in the High School. Lawrence, Kan.: University of Kansas Publications, School of Education, February, 1960.

WITTY, PAUL and BRINK, W. G. "Remedial Reading Practices in the Secondary School," *Journal of Educational Psychology*, XL (April, 1949), 193–205.

APPENDIX A

Professional Materials for the Teacher of Reading

FAY, LEO. *Reading in the High School: What Research Says to the Teacher.* Bulletin No. 11, National Education Association. Washington, D.C.: The Association, 1956.

GRAY, WILLIAM S. (comp. and ed.). *Improving Reading in Content Fields.* Supplementary Educational Monographs, No. 62. Chicago: University of Chicago Press, 1947.

———. *Improving Reading in All Curriculum Areas.* Supplementary Educational Monographs, No. 76. Chicago: University of Chicago Press, 1952.

HART, ARCHIBALD, and LEJEUNE, F. ARNOLD. *The Latin Key to Better English.* New York: E. P. Dutton Co., 1956.

HARDY, LOIS LYNN. *How to Study in High School.* Palo Alto, Calif.: Pacific Books, 1954.

HAYAKAWA, S. I. *Language in Thought and Action.* New York: Harcourt, Brace and Co., 1949.

Improvement of Reading in Secondary Schools. Austin: Texas Education Agency, 1955.

Instructional Guide for the Teaching of Reading Improvement, Junior and Senior High Schools. Los Angeles: Los Angeles City School District, 1953.

JEWETT, ARNO (ed.). *Improving Reading in the Junior High School.* Bulletin No. 10, U.S. Department of Health, Education, and Welfare. Washington, D.C.: Government Printing Office, 1957.

LAIRD, CHARLTON. *The Miracle of Language.* Cleveland: World Publishing Co., 1953.

LAIRD, HELENE, and LAIRD, CHARLTON. *The Tree of Language.* Cleveland: World Publishing Co., 1957.

LAZAR, MAY (ed.). *Retarded Reader in the Junior High School.* New York: Bureau of Educational Research, Board of Education, City of New York, 1952.

LEESTMA, ROBERT. *Audio-Visual Materials for Teaching Reading.* Ann Arbor, Mich.: Slater's Book Store, 1954.

MATHEWS, MITFORD M. *American Words.* Cleveland: World Publishing Co., 1959.

MINTEER, CATHERINE. *Words and What They Do to You.* Evanston, Ill.: Row, Peterson, and Co., 1953.

MILLER, WARD S. *Word Wealth.* New York: Henry Holt and Co., 1958.

NORVELL, GEORGE W. *The Reading Interests of Young People.* Boston: D. C. Heath and Co., 1950.

"Reading Instruction for the Slow Learner in the Secondary School," *Bulletin of the National Association of Secondary School Principals,* XXXIV (February, 1950).

Reading in the High School and College. 47th Yearbook, National Society for the Study of Education, Part II. Chicago: University of Chicago Press, 1948.

Road to Better Reading. Albany: New York State Education Department, 1953.

ROBERTS, CLYDE. *Word Attack: A Way to Better Reading.* New York: Harcourt, Brace and Co., 1956.

ROBINSON, HELEN M. (comp. and ed.). *Developing Permanent Interests in Reading.* Supplementary Educational Monographs, No. 84. Chicago: University of Chicago Press, 1956.

―――. *Promoting Maximal Reading Growth among Able Learners.* Supplementary Educational Monographs, No. 81. Chicago: University of Chicago Press, 1954.

RUSSELL, DAVID H., and KARP, ETTA E. *Reading Aids through the Grades.* New York: Bureau of Publications, Teachers College, Columbia University, 1954.

SONDEL, BESS. *The Humanity of Words, A Primer of Semantics.* Cleveland: World Publishing Co., 1958.

STRANG, RUTH, and BRACKEN, DOROTHY K. *Making Better Readers.* Boston: D. C. Heath and Co., 1957.

STRANG, RUTH; McCULLOUGH, CONSTANCE; and TRAXLER, ARTHUR. *Problems in the Improvement of Reading*. New York: McGraw-Hill Book Co., 1955.

STEWART, L. JANE; HELLER, FRIEDA M.; and ALBERTY, ELSIE J. *Improving Reading in the Junior High School*. New York: Appleton-Century-Crofts, Inc., 1957.

"Teaching Reading for the Gifted in Secondary Schools," *Bulletin of the National Association of Secondary School Principals*, XXIX (October, 1955).

What We Know about High School Reading. Champaign, Ill.: National Council of Teachers of English, 1957–58.

WITTY, PAUL, and RATZ, MARGARET. *A Developmental Reading Program for Grades 6 through 9*. Chicago: Science Research Associates, 1956.

WOOD, EVELYN NIELSEN, and BARROWS, MARJORIE WESCOTT. *Reading Skills*. New York: Henry Holt and Co., 1958.

APPENDIX B

Workbooks, Texts, and Series of Readers; Audio-Visual Materials for the Improvement of Secondary School Reading

These materials may be used for the improvement of reading skills of junior high school and senior high school students. L: indicates the approximate level of difficulty by grade placement; I: indicates the range of the interest level.

Aladdin Books. American Book Co. L:2–10 I:1–12
Variety of titles of interest to teen-agers.

All about Books. Random House. L:3–4 I:5–12
Science and social studies content.

American Adventure Series. Wheeler. L:2–6 I:3–12
Lives of famous Americans; particularly interesting to the teen-age boy.

Around the World Series. Macmillan. L:4 I:4–8
Geography content; trips around the world.

Basic Science Education. Row, Peterson, L:1–6 I:1–9
Pamphlets of 36 pages each; science content.

Basic Reading Skills for Junior High School Use. Scott, Foresman. L:6–8 I:6–10
Practice manual for development of word-attack, word-meaning skills; comprehension skills; reference skills.

Basic Reading Skills for High School Use. Scott, Foresman. L:9–12 I:9–12
Practice manual for development of word-attack, word-meaning skills; comprehension skills; reference skills.

Be a Better Reader Series, Book I–VI. Prentice-Hall. L:6–12 I:6–12
Excellent practice material for development of all reading skills; interesting, challenging selections, carefully graded.

Better Reading and Study Habits. World Book. L:7–12 I:7–14
Excellent suggestions and exercises for the improvement of
reading and study skills.

Building Reading Skills. McCormick-Mathers. L:3–8 I:3–12
Series of 6 workbooks, designed to improve word-attack, word-
meaning, and comprehension skills.

Childhood of Famous Americans. Bobbs-Merrill. L:4–5 I:3–12
Over 100 titles; biographies of famous Americans, correlated
with social science units.

Deep Sea Adventures Series. Harr-Wagner. L:1–5 I:1–12
Wonderfully illustrated, well-written adventures that appeal
to small children and teen-agers alike.

Developing Reading Skills. Laidlaw. L:4–6 I:4–12
Three workbooks, A,B,C; designed to give practice in word
recognition and meaning, comprehension, and dictionary
skills.

Dolch Pleasure Reading Series. Garrard Press. L:1–4 I:1–12
Careful development of vocabulary; interesting collections of
folk tales, fables, short subjects.

Every-Reader Series; Junior Every-Reader Series. Webster. L:4–5
I:3–12
Well-loved tales; graded classics.

Easy Reading Series. Houghton Mifflin. L:1–8 I:1–10
Interesting content and careful vocabulary development.

Famous Stories. Benjamin Sanborn. L:4–5 I:4–12
Familiar classics, adapted for the retarded reader.

Gates-Peardon Practice Exercises in Reading. Bureau of Publications, Teachers College, Columbia University. L:6–8 I:6–12
Short exercises to aid in improvement of reading skills.

Globe Adapted Classics. Globe. L:4–6 I:4–12
Familiar classics, carefully adapted for the reluctant reader.

Harr-Wagner Series. Harr-Wagner. L:4–6 I:4–12
Three titles of high interest to high school students.

Junior Library Series. Morrow. L:3–6 I:4–12
Wide selection of interests and titles.

Landmark Books. Random House. L:4–6 I:4–12

Outstanding selection of historical events, expertly written for young people. Records and filmstrips are available for correlation with many of the titles.

Let's Read Series. Henry Holt. L:6–12 I:6–12

Four titles, including highly interesting stories designed to aid in the development of wide reading skills.

My Hobby Is Series. Hart. L:5–6 I:5–12

Hobbies interestingly presented.

North Star Series. Houghton Mifflin. L:4–6 I:4–12

One of the most significant series published recently, written by outstanding American authors.

Piper Books. Houghton Mifflin. L:2–4 I:2–8

Biographies well written; interesting to the older teen-ager who cannot read well.

Practice Readers. Webster. L:1–6 I:1–10

Series of workbooks, with short exercises designed for skills development.

Reading and Thinking Series. Macmillan. L:7–10 I:7–12

Series of three books, including experiences, practices, and problems in reading and thinking.

Reading Adventures Series. Merrill. L:1–6 I:1–10

Three readers, designed as workbooks, well illustrated and carefully developed to give practice in basic skills.

Reading Essentials Series. Steck. L:1–8 I:1–12

Readers in workbook format, interesting and provocative.

Reading for Meaning Series. Lippincott. L:4–12 I:4–14

A separate workbook for each grade from 4 through 12.

Reading Skills Builders. Reader's Digest. L:2–6 I:2–12

Short selections of contemporary interest, well written.

Real People Series. Row, Peterson. L:5 I:4–10

Biographies, in pamphlet form, of famous people.

Rochester Occupational Reading Series. L:3–6 I:3–12

Series of books dealing with familiar occupations and providing practice in skills development. Each book is written at three different levels for use with multigroup class.

Signature Books. Grosset and Dunlap. L:5–6 I:5–12
  Biographies of famous people.
Simplified Classics. Scott, Foresman. L:4–6 I:4–12
  Good selection of classics, adapted for slow readers.
SRA Better Reading Books. Science Research Associates. L:5–10
  I:5–12
  Short selections, in three separate volumes, designed to aid the
  student in checking his own progress in rate and compre-
  hension.
Teen Age Tales. Heath. L:6–10 I:6–12
  Excellent selections written for the junior and senior high
  school student; nine books available in 1960.
Triple Title Series. Franklin Watts. L:5–9 I:5–12
  Collections of stories of high interest for the teen-age student.
Way of Life Series. Row, Peterson. L:5–6 I:5–12
  Discussions of vocational interests.
Westminster Books. Westminster Press. L:6–12 I:6–14
  A wide selection of titles, particularly written for the junior
  and high school student.
We Were There Series. Grosset and Dunlap. L:4–5 I:4–12
  Events of history related by people who experienced them.
Wings for Reading. Heath. L:7–9 I:7–12
  Three titles; interesting selection of stories.
Winston Adventure Series. Winston. L:4–6 I:4–10
  Events in history, well written.
World Landmark Series. Random House. L:4–6 I:4–12
  Superior writing; events in world history.

Audio-Visual Aids

Filmstrip Reading Series. Pacific Productions. L:2–12 I:2–12
  Series of forty-one color filmstrips on use of the dictionary,
  reading for understanding, phonetic analysis, structural analysis, and efficient use of books.
Phrase Reading Series. C-B Educational Films. L:6–14 I:6–adult

Series of fifteen practice films and one introductory film, designed to aid the student in the development of speed and comprehension. A student's manual, containing correlated readings and exercises, is available.

Keys to Reading. C-B Educational Films. L:7–12 I:7–adult
Three sound films, developing the significance of words, phrases and sentences, and paragraphs in reading with full understanding.

Pathways to Reading. C-B Educational Films. L:4–10 I:4–12
Five sound films, designed to stimulate interest in reading and to give the student information on how to read better.

APPENDIX C

Lists of Books for Retarded Readers

Annotated Bibliography of Selected Books with High Interest and Low Vocabulary Level. Curriculum Bulletin No. 22, Indianapolis Public Schools, 1954.

This list is divided into two sections: Section I lists books in subject or interest areas; Section II lists series of books which are graded for specified interest and vocabulary levels.

BERGLUND, ALBERT O. (comp.). *Easy Books Interesting to Children of Junior High School Age Who Have Reading Difficulties.* Winnetka, Ill.: Winnetka Educational Press, 1948.

BERNER, ELSA R., and SACRA, MABEL (eds.). *A Basic Book Collection for Junior High Schools.* Chicago: American Library Association, 1950.

Basic books for the junior high school library, listed by subject areas. Includes, also, short story collections and magazines for the junior high school.

Books for You, A List for Leisure Reading for Use by Students in Senior High Schools. Champaign, Ill.: National Council of Teachers of English, 1956.

Excellent book list for high school students, based on purposes for reading.

CARPENTER, HELEN McCRACKEN. *Gateways to American History: An Annotated Graded List of Books for Slow Learners in Junior High School.* New York: H. W. Wilson Co., 1952.

Books are annotated by historical period and by topic.

CLARK, MARGARET MARY (comp.). *Adventuring with Books.* Champaign, Ill.: National Council of Teachers of English, 1950.

Primarily for elementary children, this list should be useful to

245

the teacher who is searching for high-interest materials for the retarded reader in the high school.

DUNN, ANITA E., and Others. *Fare for the Reluctant Reader.* Albany: New York State College for Teachers, 1952.

An indispensable aid to the teacher of reading in the junior or senior high school.

FROGNER, ELLEN (ed.). *Your Reading, A List for Junior High Schools.* Champaign, Ill.: National Council of Teachers of English, 1954.

Listed by interest areas, each book has been carefully selected; very easy and challenging books are specially marked.

HILL, MARGARET KEYSER (comp.). *Bibliography of Reading Lists for Retarded Readers.* Iowa City: State University of Iowa, 1953.

Compilations of books with interest content higher than actual reader level.

HOBSON, CLOY S., and HAUGH, OSCAR M. *Materials for the Retarded Reader.* Lawrence, Kan.: School of Education, University of Kansas, 1954.

A descriptive list of books which may be used with retarded readers; annotations are excellent.

JACOBS, LELAND B. (comp.). *A Bibliography of Books for Children.* Bulletin No. 37 of the A.C.E.I. Washington 5, D.C.: Association for Childhood Education International, 1952.

Excellent bibliography, with books listed in interest areas; recommendations are made for age level at which book is most useful.

ROBINSON, HELEN M. (ed.). "Remedial Reading Materials and Equipment," *Clinical Studies in Reading, II.* Supplementary Educational Monographs, No. 77. Chicago: University of Chicago Press, 1953.

Careful selection of items and good annotations.

ROOS, JEAN CAROLYN. *Patterns in Reading.* Chicago: American Library Association, 1954.

Includes entries under 100 reading interests of youth; books are listed for junior high school students through adulthood.

SPACHE, GEORGE. *Good Books for Poor Readers*. Gainesville, Fla.: University of Florida, 1954.

The most extensive bibliography of its kind currently available.

STRANG, RUTH M., and Others. *Gateways to Readable Books*. New York: H. W. Wilson Co., 1952.

Several hundred titles for the high school student who is a poor reader.

SULLIVAN, HELEN BLAIR (comp.). *High Interest Low Vocabulary Booklist*. Boston: Educational Clinic, Boston University School of Education, 1952.

A superior source for the teacher of reading, this booklist gives both vocabulary level and interest level of each entry.

WARNER, DOROTHY (comp.). *Bibliography of Reading Materials for the Mentally Retarded on the Secondary Level*. Topeka, Kan.: Division of Special Education, State Department of Public Instruction, 1954.

Brief list, but careful selection of materials for the special education class.

APPENDIX D

Phonetic Principles

These phonetic principles, which apply to the pronunciation of words, are of help to the teacher and the student:

1. The sounds of single consonants may vary:

   s: *s*ing, wa*s*
   g: *g*oing, *g*em
   c: has the sound of *s* when followed by *e* or *i:* cease, cigarette
   has the sound of *k* when followed by *a, o,* or *u:* came, copy, cute

2. When two consonants are combined, one of them may always be silent: *g*nu, *k*nife, *p*neumonia, wa*l*k, ca*t*ch; occasionally, both consonants may be silent: thou*gh*, brou*ght*.

3. Some sounds are represented by many different symbols: gra*d*uate, *j*ump, we*dg*e, ma*g*ic

4. When a double consonant appears, one of the consonants is silent: pil*l*ow, let*t*er.

5. Some vowels are silent:

   Final *e* on a word is silent and usually prolongs the sound of the preceding vowel: bone, tame, lime, dune
   When two vowels appear together in a word or syllable, the first vowel is usually long in sound and the second vowel is usually silent: coat, train, meat, ream, beet

6. When there is but one vowel in a syllable or word, the sound of that vowel is usually short: f*u*n, s*i*mple, p*a*mphl*e*t

7. When a vowel appears at the end of a syllable or word, it usually has its long sound: r*e*lief, pr*o*cession, appr*o*priate

8. Some vowels form syllables by themselves: vi-*o*-lin.
9. A single vowel followed by *r* in a word or syllable is usually affected by the sound of the *r*: w*o*rk, sh*i*rt, ch*a*ra*c*te*r*.

Structural Analysis

These principles may be applied when adding inflectional endings and recognizing variants of words:

1. Most inflectional variants are formed by adding endings with no change in the root word: talking, shouted, watches, seeing, books.
2. When the root word ends in a final *e*, the *e* is usually dropped before an ending that begins with a vowel: coming, raked (the *e* has been dropped and *ed* has been added). When root words end in *ce* and *ge*, the *e* is retained when an ending beginning with *a* or *o* is added: courageous, peaceable.
3. If a syllable or root word ends in a single consonant preceded by a vowel, the consonant may be doubled when an ending is added: stopped, whipped, fanning. Note that this principle applies only if the enlarged word is accented on the final syllable: benefit, bene*fi*ted.
4. Words ending in *f* or *fe* usually form their plurals by changing the *f* to a *v* and adding the plural endings: knives, scarves.
5. When a word ends with *y*, preceded by a consonant, the *y* is usually changed to an *i* before an ending is added: ladies, cried, emptied. If the *y* is preceded by a vowel, there is no change in the root word when an ending is added: chimneys, allayed.

Principles of Syllabication

1. Every syllable in a word contains a sounded vowel: a-bun-dant, prin-ci-ple
2. Often a vowel forms a syllable by itself: vi-o-lin
3. When there are two consonants between two vowels, the syl-

lable division is usually made between the consonants: af-ter, chap-ter.

4. When a word ends in *le*, preceded by a consonant, the consonant usually is included in the last syllable: syl-la-ble, a-ble

5. When a double consonant appears between two vowels. the second consonant is usually silent: let-*t*er lit-*t*er

6. When words end in *-tion* or *-sion,* the accent usually falls on the next to the last syllable: gradua′tion, suspen′sion

7. When a syllable ends in a consonant, the vowel is usually short: r*a*f-ter; when a syllable ends in a vowel, the vowel is usually long: d*e*-sign.

8. When the suffix *ed* is added to a word ending in *t* or *d,* a separate syllable is formed: want-ed, land-ed.

Table of Affixes and Roots *

Prefixes	Meaning	Example
a-, an-	not, without	atypical, anarchy
ab-	away from, off from, away	abdicate
ad-	to, toward	admit
ambi-	both	ambivalence
amphi-	both, around, about	amphitheater
ana-	up, backward, excessively	anachronism
ante-	before, preceding, prior to	antecedent
anti-	against	antipathy
auto-	self	automobile
be-	completely	bedecked
by-	near, secondary, incidental	bypath
cata-, cath-	down, against, in accordance	catalogue
circum-	around	circumspect
com-, con-, col-, cor-, co-	together with	correlate
contra-	against	contradict
de-	down, from, away, out of	depose
dia-	through, across, between	diameter
dis-	apart from, reversing	dissuade

* J. B. Stroud, R. B. Ammons, and H. A. Bamman, *Improving Reading Ability* (New York: Appleton-Century-Crofts, Inc., 1955). Reproduced by permission of the publisher.

Table of Affixes and Roots (*continued*)

Prefixes	*Meaning*	*Example*
ec-, ex-	out of	exodus, exit
en-	in	enamored
epi-	upon, beside, among, over	epigram
eu-	well, good	eulogy
ex-	out of, beyond, without, thoroughly, formerly	exhale, ex-governor
fore-	in front of (position, time)	forecast
hyper-	over	hypersensitive
hypo-	under, beneath	hypodermic
in-, im-, il-, ir-	into, not (as an adjective)	infuse, irrevocable
inter-, intro-, intra-	between, among, together, within	intercede, intramural, introduce
meta-	with, after, over, beyond	metamorphosis
mis-	wrong, wrongly	misinterpret
miso-	hatred of	misogynist
ob-, oc-, of-, op-	toward, to, against, upon	oppose, obdurate
omni-	all	omnibus
pan-	all	panacea
para-	beside, beyond	paragraph
per-	throughout, completely	permit
peri-	around	periscope
poly-	many	polychrome
post-	after	postponed
pre-	before	preview
pro-	forward	proceed
re-	back, again	reduce
se-	aside	secede
sub-, suc-, suf-, sug-, sup-, sus-	under, subordinate	subterranean
super-	over, above, above in position	supercilious
syn-, sy-, sym-	with, along with, at the same time	synchronize, sympathy
trans-	across, beyond	transit
vice-	in place of	viceroy
with-	against, away	withstand
uni-, mono-	one	unilateral, monogram
bi-, di-	two	bicuspid, dialogue
tri-	three	tricycle
quadr-, tetra-	four	quadruped, tetrameter
penta-, quin-	five	pentagon, quintuplet

Table of Affixes and Roots (*continued*)

Prefixes	Meaning	Example
sex-, hexa-	six	sextant, hexagon
sept-, hepta-	seven	September, heptagon
oct-	eight	octave
nona-	nine	nonagenarian
dec-	ten	decimate
centi-	one hundred	centigrade
milli-	one thousand	millennium
kilo-	one thousand	kilocycle
multi-	many	multigraph
semi-, hemi-	half or partially, half	semiweekly, hemisphere

Common Roots (*Latin*)

Root	Meaning	Derivatives
-ag-, -act-, -ig-	move, do	agitate, actuate, exigency
-agri-	field	agriculture, agricologist
-aud-, audit-	hear	audible, auditorium
-avi-	bird	aviary, aviation
-caput-	head	capitulate, capitalize
-ced-, -cess-	move, yield	recede, proceed, secede
-cern-, -crete-	distinguish	discern, concern, discrete
-cit-	rouse or call	incite, cite
-clam-	call, cry out	clamor, declaim
-clar-	clear	clarion, clarify
-clin-	lean	decline, incline
-clud-, -claud-, -claus-	shut	claustrophobia, seclude, clause
-cord-	heart	accord, cordial
-corp-	body	corpse, corporal
-cred-	to believe	credible, credence
-cresc-, -cret-	grow, rise	crescendo, secretion
-curr-, -curs-	run	current, cursive
-dic-, -dict-	say	dictaphone, dictate, predict
-domin-	master	dominion, dominate
-duc-, -duct-	lead	conduct, ductile
-fac-, -fic-, -fact-, -fect-	to make, do	fact, factory, beneficent
-facil-	easy	facile, facility
-fer-	bear, carry	transfer, offer
-fid-	faith	fidelity, confidential
-fin-	end	finally, finish

Table of Affixes and Roots (*continued*)

Root	Meaning	Derivatives
-flect-, -flex-	bend	deflect, flexible
-fort-	strong	fortitude, discomfort
-gen-, -ject-	race	genteel, progenitor
-jac-, -ject-	hurl or throw	projectile, javelin, eject
-jun-, -junct-	join	adjunct, junction
-laud-, -laudat-	praise	applause
-let-, -lect-	gather, choose, read	collect, elect, legible, lecture
-legis-, -lex-	law	legal, legislature
-loqu-, -locut-	speak	loquacious, elocution
-lux-, -luc-	light	lucidity, elucidate
-magn-	great	magnificent, magnanimous
-mal-	bad	malevolent, malediction
-man-	hand	manipulate, manual
-mit-, -miss-	send	transmit, missile
-mov-, -mot-	set in motion	mobile, move, motor
-nov-, -novus-	new	novel, renovation
-offic-	duty	official, officer
-pac-	peace	pacify, pacific
-par-, -parat-	make ready	preparation, prepare
-pel-, -puls-	urge, drive	propel, expulsion
-pend-, -pens-	hang, weigh	pendant, pensive
-pet-	seek, ask	petition, repeat
-plen-	full	plenty, replenish
-plic-, -plex-	bend, fold	plexiglas, duplicate
-pon-, -pos-	place, put	oppose, postpone
-salu-	healthy	salutary, salubrious
-sci-	know	conscience, science
-scrib-, -script-	write	describe, ascribe
-sed-, -sess-	set	sedentary, session
-sen-	old	senile, senior
-sent-, -sens-	feel	sentiment, sensitive
-sequo-, -secut-	follow	sequence, persecute
-solv-, -solut-	loosen	solvent, solution
-spec-, -spect-	look	spectator, specimen
-spir-, -spirit-	breathe	expire, inspire
-sta-	stand firm	stable, stationary
-stru-, -struct-	build	construe, instruct, construct
-sum-, -sumpt-	spend, take up	consume, presume
-tect-	cover	protect, detective
-ten-	hold	tenacious, tentacle
-tend-, -tens-	stretch	extend, tendency, tension

Table of Affixes and Roots (*continued*)

Root	Meaning	Derivatives
-tort-	to twist	distort, extort
-tract-	draw	tractor, extract
-ven-, -vent-	come	convene, venture, convention
-ver-	true	verily, veritable
-vert-, -vers-	turn	vertical, converse, reverse
-vinc-, -vict-	conquer	convince, victory
-viv-, -vit-	live, life	vivacious, survive, vitality
-vid-, -vis-	see	evident, provision
-voc-	call	vocation, invoke
-vol-	wish	voluntary, volition

Common Roots (*Greek*)

Root	Meaning	Derivatives
-anthrop-	man	anthropology, philanthropy
-arch-	first, chief	monarch, archbishop
-aster-	star	astrology, asterisk
-bibl-	book	Bible, bibliography
-bio-	life	biography, biology
-chrom-	color	chromatic, kodachrome
-chron-	time	chronometer, chronological
-crypt-	secret	cryptic, cryptogram
-dem-	people	democracy, epidemic
-derm-	skin	dermatology, epidermis
-dox-	opinion	orthodox, paradox
-dynam-	power	dynamo, dynamic
-gam-	marriage	polygamy, misogamy
-gen-	birth	progeny, eugenics
-geo-	earth	geopolitics, geography
-gyn-	woman	gynecology, misogynist
-graph-, -gram-	write, written	photograph, monogram, program
-hetero-	different	heterogeneous, heterodox
-homo-	same	homogeneous, homologous
-hydr-	water	hydrometer, hydrate
-lith-	stone	lithography, monolith
-log-, -logy-	speech, word, study	catalogue, astrology

Table of Affixes and Roots (*continued*)

Root	Meaning	Derivatives
-mega-	great	megacephalic, megalomania
-metr-	measure	metronome, thermometer
-micro-	small	miscroscope, microphone
-nom-, -nomy-	law	economy, astronomy
-path-	feeling, suffering	sympathy, psychopathy
-phan-	show	diaphanous, cellophane
-phil-	love	philologist, philosopher
-phon-	sound	phonetics, dictaphone
-photo-	light	photogenic, photograph
-physio-	nature	physiology, physics
-pod-	foot	chiropody, tripod
-polis-	city	metropolis, political
-psych-	mind	psychology, psychic
-pyr-	fire	pyromaniac, pyre
-scop-	see	stethoscope, microscope
-soph-	wise	philosopher, sophistry
-tele-	far	telegraphy, telescope
-the-	god	atheist, pantheism
-tom-	cut	epitome, anatomy
-trop-	turning	heliotrope, tropic, tropism
-zo-	animal	zodiac, zoology

Suffixes

Suffix	Meaning	Example
-able, -ible, -ble	capable of, worthy of	noticeable, voluble
-acious, -cious	tending to, or having the quality of	pugnacious, capacious
-acy, -cy, -age, -al	state of being, or quality, state of, pertaining to	accuracy, hesitancy, marriage, hostage, marital, causal
-an, -ian	designating or belong to	artisan, guardian
-ance, -ancy	state, quality, act or condition	persistence, brilliance, agency
-ant, -ent, -ar, -er, -or	one who acts	registrant, student, bursar, teacher, doctor
-ard, -art	one who acts ignominiously or does something excessively	braggart, drunkard, coward
-ar, -ary	pertaining to, connected with	secular, elementary

Table of Affixes and Roots (*continued*)

Suffix	Meaning	Example
-ate, -ite, -cle, -cule, -dom, -eer, -ier	possessing or being, diminutives, a state or condition, one who acts	favorite, incapacitate, particle, molecule, martyrdom, serfdom, furrier, auctioneer
-en	made of, to make of, suggesting smallness	leaden, lessen, weaken
-ette, -ess, -trix, -esque, -ese,	small or diminutive, one who acts, in the manner of	dinette, statuette, waitress, aviatrix, picturesque, grotesque, journalese, celanese,
-ferous, -fid, -fix	of, or relating to, bringing, yielding, making or causing	odoriferous, carboniferous, pacific, soporific
-ful, -fly, -efy, -ify, -hood	full of, abounding in, to make, state of	cheerful, masterful, defy, rarefy, testify, childhood, neighborhood
-ic, -ical	of, pertaining to, similar or like	moronic, historic, historical
-ice, -ile, -il, -ine (fem.)	act, quality, or state pertaining to, like one who acts	justice, cowardice, servile, civil, heroine
-ion	state, condition or act of	insurrection, exhaustion
-ish	acting like, in the nature of acting like, in the nature of, or similar to	impish, selfish, mannish
-ism	art of, philosophy of, practice of	liberalism, Americanism
-ist	one who acts	philanthropist, atheist
-ity, -ty	condition, state or degree of	gratuity, plenty
-ive	having the nature of, giving or tending toward	imaginative, collective
-ize, -ise, -le, -el, -lent, -ulent	to make into, to practice, diminutiveness, abounding in	mesmerize, familiarize, teakettle, icicle, violent, fraudulent
-less	without, beyond the	fearless, useless
-ly	similar in manner	dearly, fully, carefully
-ment	state, quality, or act of	detriment, entanglement
-mony, -ness	abstract condition, state or condition	acrimony, ceremony, strictness, fairness
-ory	of, pertaining to, place of, or for	auditory, prohibitory, offertory

Table of Affixes and Roots (*continued*)

Suffix	Meaning	Example
-ose, -ous	state or quality	comatose, furious
-ship	state or quality, art or skill	courtship, partnership
-some	like or same	bothersome, quarrelsome
-ster (masculine), -stress (feminine)	one who acts	teamster, songstress
-try, -tude	art or profession of, state or quality	foresty, ministry, platitude, aptitude
-ure	act or process, result of	adventure, tenure

APPENDIX E

Interest Inventory *

Name _____ Boy _____ Girl _____

Class (circle one)   9   10   11   12   _____ School

For what field is your high school work preparing you?

Vocational _____	Marriage _____
College _____	Secretarial or business _____
Military _____	Undecided _____

MAGAZINES	MAGAZINES
a) What magazines do you read regularly?	a) _____
b) To which do you or the family subscribe?	b) _____
c) Which do you purchase at the newsstand regularly?	c) _____

NEWSPAPERS	NEWSPAPERS
a) What newspapers do you read regularly?	a) _____
b) Which section of the newspaper do you always read? List your first three choices: 1, 2, 3.	b) 1) society___ 5) movie guide___ 2) comics___ 3) sports___ 6) advertise- 4) drama___ ments___

* Courtesy of Ben Leafe. M.A. Thesis, Sacramento State College, 1958.

NEWSPAPERS

NEWSPAPERS

7) front
   page___

8) TV-
   radio___

9) edito-
   rials___

10) music &
    records___

11) classi-
    fied___

12) letters
    to the
    editor___

13) syndicated columns___

BOOKS

BOOKS

a) Name the books you have read during the past year (not more than five).

a) _____
   _____
   _____
   _____

b) Which of these was your favorite and why did you like it?

b) _____
   _____
   _____

c) Who suggested that you read this book?

c) Mother___   Father___
   Friend___   Myself___
   Librarian___   Church
   Teacher___   leader___

d) On whom have you relied most for suggestions of books which you have read?

d) _____
   _____
   _____

e) Comic books—

e) 1) Do you buy them? ___
   2) Do you read them on newsstands? ___
   3) Do you borrow them ___

GENERAL QUESTIONS

a) If you had your choice, what type or types of books would you read? Make

a) 1) Poetry___   4) Careers___
   2) Sports___   5) Animal___
   3) Romance___   6) Comics___

GENERAL QUESTIONS

three choices—1, 2, 3, in
order of your preference.

7) Mystery___ 11) Tech-
8) Science   nical___
   fiction___   12) Histori-
9) Biogra-   cal___
   phy___   13) Reli-
10) Travel-   gious___
    Explora-   14) Classical
    tion___   fiction___

b) Do you or your parents
belong to a book club?
If so, which one?

b) Yes___   No___

_____

c) What book have you read
which was suggested by a
TV program?

c) _____
_____
_____

d) What book have you read
which was suggested by a
movie?

d) _____
_____
_____

e) What book have you read
which was suggested by a
radio program?

e) _____
_____
_____

f) What book has been your
favorite of all time?

f) _____
_____

g) Why is this your favorite?

g) _____

h) What book have you read
which you really disliked?

h) _____
_____

i) Why did you dislike it?

i) _____
_____

Index